THE MOVERS & SHAKERS OF
VICTORIAN
England

PJ Harris

**A WHO'S WHO OF HISTORY'S MOST GIFTED,
FAMOUS AND INFLUENTIAL PEOPLE**

ENGLISH HERITAGE

THINK
BOOKS

A Think Book for English Heritage
First published in 2006 by

Think Publishing
The Pall Mall Deposit
124-128 Barlby Road
London W10 6BL

Distributed in the United States and Canada by
Sterling Publishing Co., Inc.
387 Park Avenue South
New York, NY 10016-8810

Text: © Think Publishing 2006
Layout: © Think Publishing 2006

Published in association with
English Heritage
Kemble Drive
Swindon SN2 2GZ

Author: PJ Harris
Editors: Melanie Green and Emma Jones
Sub editors: Victoria Chow, Rica Dearman and Marion Thompson
Design: Lou Millward and Mark Evans
Cover design: Jes Stanfield

ISBN-10: 1-90562-406-9
ISBN-13: 978-90562-406-5

Printed and bound in Great Britain by William Clowes Ltd, Beccles, Suffolk
Cover image: Mary Evans Picture Library; Corbis

With thanks to:

Adele Campbell, Rob Richardson and Rene Rodgers

❧

'I contend that we are the finest race in the world;
and that the more of the world we inhabit,
the better it is for the human race.'

Cecil Rhodes
(father of the British empire of South Africa)

✃

CONTENTS

Chapter I
Rulers, princes & potentates
9

Chapter II
Battlers for men's souls
21

Chapter III
Heroes & imperialists
29

Chapter IV
Eccentric souls
41

Chapter V
Pioneers of progress
53

Chapter VI
Victorian heroines
65

Chapter VII
The literary elite
79

Chapter VIII
Moulders of young minds
95

Chapter IX
Greasepaint monkeys, ne'er do wells & the hoi polloi
111

Chapter X
Makers of music
123

Chapter XI
Artistic visionaries
135

Chapter XII
Good sports
149

CHAPTER I

RULERS, PRINCES & POTENTATES

Queen Victoria's reign (1837–1901) was the longest in British history – and one of the most successful. Despite troubles in Crimea, India and Ireland, the Victorian era was a long period of peace and economic consolidation. Politically, it was also a time of outstanding statesmen, with political colossi, such as Lord Melbourne, Lord Palmerston, Disraeli and Lord Gladstone, vying for power in the House of Commons. During Victoria's reign, rule constantly jumped between the Whigs (later the Liberals) and the Tories, with Rosebery and Aberdeen in power once; Melbourne, Peel, Russell, Palmerston and Disraeli twice; Derby and Salisbury three times; and Gladstone four times.

QUEEN VICTORIA and PRINCE ALBERT
(1819–1901 and 1819–1861)
A love match made in Germany

Alexandrina Victoria was born on 24 May 1819, the only child of Edward, Duke of Kent, and Victoria Maria Louisa of Saxe-Coburg, the sister of King Leopold of Belgium. Her father died when she was just eight months old, and as a result, Victoria spoke only German (her mother's native tongue) until she was three. She became queen in 1840 and reigned for more than 63 years, despite seven assassination attempts: the first in 1840, when she was pregnant with her first child, and the last in 1882.

Victoria's was a reign marked by a great expansion of the British empire and the social and economic upheaval of the Industrial Revolution, but the queen is remembered just as clearly for her personal life. Victoria met and married her cousin Prince Albert of Saxe-Coburg in 1837, resulting in nine children and one of the most celebrated of all royal partnerships.

Not just the queen's consort, Albert also became an important political adviser to Victoria, notably guiding her on the subjects of industrialisation and child labour in Britain. He also planned and helped to manage the Great Exhibition of 1851, the profits from which were used to build London's Royal Albert Hall and the Victoria and Albert Museum.

The prince died of typhoid fever in December 1861 and Victoria withdrew into intense mourning at Balmoral. While there, she formed a close attachment with a Scottish retainer, John Brown, and there were even rumours of a secret marriage. This mystery was heightened by her will, opened after Victoria died on 22 January 1901 at Osborne House on the Isle of Wight. In it, she asked for two sets of mementoes to be placed in her coffin: one of Albert's dressing gowns, and a piece of Brown's hair, together with a picture of him.

BENJAMIN DISRAELI
(1804–1881)
Prime minister and novelist

Another of the political colossi who bestrode mid-Victorian politics, Benjamin Disraeli abandoned a planned career in law for a life in the House of Commons and, eventually, Downing Street. Disraeli was a zealous reformer, standing during the 1830s as a Radical candidate, before finally securing election to the House of Commons as a Tory in 1837. He made little initial impact, however, and, when Prime Minister Robert Peel rejected his plea for a Cabinet post in 1841, became a trenchant critic of the Peelites and one of the leaders of the Young England faction of the Tory party.

Disraeli's first office of note was that of chancellor of the exchequer, which he held for a few months in 1852 and again in 1858 under the Earl of Derby. The Tories, however, fell from power, remaining in opposition until 1868. Returned once again to parliament in the election of that year, Disraeli took the post of prime minister with the comment: 'I have climbed to the top of the greasy pole.'

The Tory government lasted only a few months in 1868, and Disraeli did not return to power until 1874. By then he was at the height of his popularity, having won public approval, while still in opposition by proposing an electoral reform bill that extended the vote to a further one and a half million men and abolished Britain's notorious rotten boroughs. His Factory Act of

1878 cut the working week to just 56 hours in the case of women and forbade the employment of children under the age of 10.

Unsavoury speculations in Disraeli's early years left him with considerable debts and he felt compelled to marry a wealthy widow, Mary-Anne Wyndham Lewis, a dozen years his senior. Nonetheless, the marriage was a success, and when, years later, Disraeli confided to a friend that he had married for money, his wife cut in: 'Ah, but if you had to do it again, you would do it for love.' Shortage of money also compelled him to embark upon a literary career. His political novels are still widely read and the satire *Lothair*, which featured a fanatical but seductive Catholic churchman unmistakably based on Cardinal Manning (see chapter II), earned its author over £10,000.

In person, Disraeli was a celebrated charmer. Unlike his great enemy William Gladstone, he enjoyed a good relationship with Queen Victoria, whom he flattered by arranging for her to be crowned Empress of India in 1876; he was rewarded with an earldom. Even this generous act, however, was not sufficient to save the old Tory from defeat in the General Election campaign of 1880. Disraeli then decided to retire, and he died a year later.

ROBERT GASCOYNE-CECIL, 3RD MARQUESS OF SALISBURY (1830–1903)
Conservative prime minister, libertarian free-thinker

Lord Salisbury is remembered as a solid late-Victorian prime minister who spent three periods in office between 1885 and 1902, held countless positions in other leaders' governments, and led the Conservative party for decades. He should also be remembered as one of the great libertarian thinkers – especially in the US where he is renowned for encouraging the establishment of working men's associations.

Salisbury was the master of the pithy put-down and a powerful public speaker. During the reading of what he considered to be a meddlesome bill to reduce the number of window-cleaning accidents suffered by servants, he asked its proposer, Sir Charles Burrell, if he planned 'to repeal the law of gravitation by Act of Parliament'.

Salisbury first became leader of the Conservatives in the House of Lords following Benjamin Disraeli's death in 1881, although he didn't have official leadership of the whole party, which led to many divisions and disruptions. Unlike most PMs, who also took on the position of first lord of the treasury, Salisbury chose to occupy the position of foreign secretary in addition to that of prime minister. He had once noted that 'English policy is to float lazily downstream, occasionally putting out a diplomatic boathook to avoid collisions', but in his time Britain was great, the head of a global empire, and he intended it to stay that way.

On his father's death, he became one of the richest men in England, but as plain Robert Gascoyne-Cecil, he was forced to earn his living as a journalist because he married against his family's wishes in 1857. Often described by biographers as 'low born', his wife, Georgina Alderson, was in fact the daughter of a judge who presented him with seven healthy children and maintained a stable family life during his often turbulent career. He resigned from public office shortly after her death and, heartbroken, died himself a few months later.

WILLIAM GLADSTONE
(1809–1898)
Prime minister, reformer and saviour of fallen women

William Gladstone, arguably the greatest British prime minister of the 19th century, won an unprecedented four terms in Downing Street, yet divided opinion more than any other politician since. He was disliked by Queen Victoria who thought him a dangerous radical and would complain: 'He always addresses me as if I were a public meeting.' He was viewed as practically a traitor to his country by the Tories, who were dismayed by his determination to solve the age-old 'Irish Question' via the medium of Home Rule. Gladstone was nonetheless beloved by tens of thousands as the creator of a modern education system and promoter of universal male suffrage. He completed his last term as prime minister at the age of 85.

Gladstone was born in Liverpool, son of a wealthy merchant, and educated at Eton and Oxford. Entering parliament as a Tory in 1832, just a year after he came down from university, he held several ministerial posts under the reformer Sir Robert Peel, including that of chancellor of the exchequer. Always serious – 'he wrote and spoke', it was said, 'like a mad clergyman, earnest, excitable, unstoppably prolix' – he noticeably lacked lightness of touch and was admired rather than liked by colleagues.

Gladstone's policies, in this early phase of his career, remained conventional; he opposed both the abolition of slavery and factory reform, and resigned from the Cabinet rather than vote for an increase in funding for a Catholic seminary. In 1852, however, he crossed the floor of the Commons to become a Liberal, immediately being appointed chancellor of the exchequer in the Aberdeen administration, became party leader in 1867, and was elected prime minister for the first time a year later.

As prime minister, Gladstone was a reluctant imperialist, attempting to persuade other nations to support disarmament. He devoted his third and fourth periods in office to Ireland, winning the election of 1892 after campaigning on the issue, but saw two bills about Home Rule defeated in parliament. The increasing bitterness of the Irish controversy eventually threatened to split the Liberal party, and he resigned for the final time in 1894.

Gladstone's private life inspired gossip then, and does so now. Horrified by his intensely passionate nature, and disgusted by his enjoyment of pornography, he turned to flagellation in an attempt to suppress his sexuality. Gladstone's other passions were walking, tree-felling and books. Towards the end of his life, he donated £40,000 and most of his collection of books to a new library. Although by then in his late 80s, the former prime minister personally transported nearly 23,000 volumes to their new home, St Deiniol's Library in Hawarden, in a wheelbarrow.

WILLIAM LAMB, LORD MELBOURNE
(1779–1848)
Prime minister and favourite of Queen Victoria

When Victoria came to the throne in 1837, the elected prime minister was Lord Melbourne, a Whig politician who believed vehemently in the right of the aristocracy to rule. As home secretary he had suppressed the Tolpuddle Martyrs in 1834, and took numerous steps to quash the incipient Trade Union movement during his political career. As prime minister, he opposed reforms to the Poor Law, and fought vigorously to keep the Corn Laws in place. According to Queen Victoria's diary, when talking about the poor, he said: 'I wish to avoid them, I don't like them in reality and therefore I don't wish to see them represented.' She thought these wise enough words to record.

Melbourne was able to charm the young and inexperienced monarch to such an extent that she overlooked his rather bumpy marital life. Not only had he been cited in a divorce case, but a friend had also tried to extort £1,400 from him to cover up his affair with the friend's wife. Then there was his own wife, Lady Caroline Lamb, whose scandalous dalliance with Lord Byron was the talk of both high and low society for many years. Such scandals would have almost certainly hindered another man's political advancement, but Melbourne managed to navigate the gossip only slightly scathed.

In 1835, after Robert Peel, the prime minister who succeeded him, resigned shortly into his premiership following parliamentary defeats, Queen Victoria persuaded Melbourne to serve a further two years. She seemed genuinely to enjoy his company, often keeping him behind after official business for a chat. In due course she gave him apartments at Windsor Castle, and uncomfortable rumours began to circulate that they might marry, even though he was 40 years older. He fell from favour for opposing her marriage to Prince Albert, but later said that his years serving her were the happiest of his life.

SIR ROBERT PEEL
(1788–1850)
Prime minister and creator of the Peelers,
Britain's first police force

Robert Peel, son of a wealthy Lancastrian factory owner, entered parliament at the age of 21 when his father bought him a seat – not an unusual start in politics at the time. Although he was twice prime minister, Peel is best remembered for his term as home secretary, when he established London's first police force, coining the term 'bobby' in the process.

His metropolitan police force first stepped onto London's streets on 29 September 1829. At first there were 1,000 'bobbies' (or 'Peelers'), a figure that soon rose to 3,000. However, their early years were hard. Many Londoners resented the tax levied to pay for the police, who they nicknamed 'Raw Lobsters', and by the time Victoria came to the throne, only 600 of the original 3,000 policemen were still in the force.

Despite being an innovator when it came to crime, most of Peel's political career is notable for his opposition to bills, beginning with the Catholic Emancipation Act. Always quick to object or resign when the turbulent shifting of power between Whigs and Tories leaned towards policies he could not agree with, he held no office between 1830 and 1841, apart from heading up the temporary 'hundred days' government after Lord Melbourne's government fell in 1834.

In 1841, he finally became prime minister on his own terms, and formed a government that included seven future or former prime ministers, including the Duke of Wellington, William Gladstone and Benjamin Disraeli. Following the repeal of the Corn Laws, which kept prices high for British farmers, Peel resigned for the last time in 1846. He was killed four years later from injuries sustained when his horse fell on him.

❦

ARCHIBALD PRIMROSE,
5TH EARL OF ROSEBERY
(1847–1929)
Liberal imperialist whose childhood dreams all came true

As a student at Eton and Oxford University, Archibald Primrose, heir to the Scottish earldom of Rosebery, decided to dedicate his life to the attainment of three goals: he wanted to marry an heiress, become prime minister and own a Derby-winning racehorse. He achieved all three. Primrose married Hannah de Rothschild, daughter of one of the richest bankers in Europe and inheritor of a £2 million fortune, in 1878. The Derby win followed: Ladas II triumphed in 1894. And in the same year, Primrose was moved up to the position of prime minister in succession to his fellow Liberal, William Gladstone.

Elevated to the earldom on attaining his majority in 1868, and thenceforth better known as Rosebery, the future prime minister had already gravitated towards the right of the party, eventually emerging as leader of a Liberal imperialist faction that supported the Boer War and opposed Irish Home Rule. He was the author of the description of the British empire as 'a commonwealth of nations'. In the course of the 1890s, the Liberal party split over these issues and never quite recovered its former dominance. Consequently, Rosebery's tenure as prime minister was far from successful. He found it hard to muster sufficient support for his more bellicose policies among his own party, and the House of Lords, dominated by Conservative peers, blocked almost all of his legislation.

Rosebery resigned as prime minister in 1895, after little more than a year, and as party leader in 1896. He then lived for over 30 years after his resignation. His last request, on his deathbed, was to hear the 'Eton Boating Song' for a final time before he passed away.

❧

LORD JOHN RUSSELL
(1792–1878)
Prime minister and electoral reformer

O f all the Victorian prime ministers, Lord Russell is by far the
least well known, and yet he drove through many important acts
during both his stints as prime minister. He was overshadowed by the
more flamboyant political figures of the day, both in terms of character
and stature; he was little over five foot four inches and weighed only
eight stone.

Born into the highest echelons of the British aristocracy (the Russell
family were among the richest handful of aristocratic landowning families
in the country), the future prime minister was generous in spirit from his
youth. At the age of 14 he wrote in his diary: 'What a pity that he who
steals a penny loaf should be hung, whilst he who steals thousands of
the public money should be acquitted.' He entered parliament in 1813,
joining the Society of Friends of the People in Parliament, which was a
Whig reform group aimed at giving ordinary people more representation.
When the Whigs came into power in 1830, Russell was responsible for
drafting the Electoral Reform Bill of 1832, which sought to double the
size of the electorate.

After Sir Robert Peel's resignation, Russell became prime minister in
1846 and stayed in power for six years. But his early premiership was
blighted by ineffectual action in response to the great Irish famine of
1846–1851, and indecision over the Crimean War cost him the leadership
of his party. After forming a second, unsuccessful government for only
a year (1865–1866), Russell retired to the House of Lords, where he
continued to speak out for the rights of the common man up until his
death in 1878.

꒰ꂦ꒱

EDWARD GEORGE STANLEY, 14TH EARL OF DERBY
(1799–1869)
Prime minister and longest-serving leader of the Conservative party

Despite being elected prime minister three times, the Earl of Derby is regarded as a weak and languid leader whose ministries were dominated by the policies of Benjamin Disraeli. His first term in 1852 was far from successful – dissolved within a matter of months, making way for a Peelite-Whig coalition. In 1858, Derby formed his second minority government upon the collapse of Lord Palmerston's first government, but it fell apart after only a year. He returned to power for the last time in 1866, after Lord Russell's second government collapsed. In early 1868, Derby retired from political life, leaving Disraeli to succeed him. By the time of his retirement, he had led the Conservative party for 22 years – to date the all-time record for the party.

HENRY JOHN TEMPLE, LORD PALMERSTON
(1784–1865)
Political survivor and late-blossoming prime minister

Writing candidly in her diary on the death of Lord Palmerston, Queen Victoria said: 'I never liked him. We had God knows! terrible trouble with him about foreign affairs. Still, as prime minister he managed affairs at home well, and behaved to me well.' The queen first clashed with Palmerston when, as foreign secretary in Lord Russell's government, he promoted policies to strengthen Britain's position as a world power, irrespective of who had to be dealt with. Victoria and Albert, having numerous relatives scattered across the ruling families of Russia and Europe, thought his energies should go into preserving the monarchy in Europe in the face of increasing Republicanism.

They also disapproved of his reputation as a ladies' man – he was reportedly discovered in the bedroom of one of Victoria's ladies-in-waiting. Lord Russell eventually sacked him, but Palmerston had his revenge a few years later when he helped bring down Russell's government.

Palmerston's start in parliament was rocky. He entered as a Tory and his first election (which he paid £1,500 to win) was challenged, so Sir Leonard Holmes used his political weight to get Palmerston elected for Newtown on the Isle of Wight, on the condition he never visit his constituency.

In 1809, at just 25, Prime Minister Spencer Perceval offered him the post of chancellor of the exchequer, but Palmerston declined, believing he was too young for the position, and became secretary at war instead. He held that post for 20 years under five successive prime ministers. Then, extraordinarily, he joined Lord Grey's Whig government as secretary of state for foreign affairs (which meant supporting the reforms he'd previously strongly opposed).

The archetypal political animal in Victorian England, Palmerston crossed and re-crossed the floor many times over the next 22 years to hold various ministerial posts, remaining well liked by his fellow MPs throughout.

Palmerston was 71 when he became prime minister in 1855. He led a second government in 1859, coming into conflict with his chancellor, William Gladstone, over electoral reform. In a letter composed following one of Gladstone's many speeches in its favour, Palmerston tartly said: 'Your speech may win Lancashire for you, although that is doubtful, but I fear it will tend to lose England for you.' Palmerston served as an MP until the year he died, aged 81.

CHAPTER II

BATTLERS FOR MEN'S SOULS

ANTHONY ASHLEY-COOPER,
7TH EARL OF SHAFTESBURY
(1801–1885)
Philanthropist, social campaigner, emancipator of children

A Tory MP, Anthony Ashley-Cooper campaigned vigorously almost from the moment of his election for factory reform, and also took an active interest in coal mining conditions, lodging houses and lunatic asylums.

Shaftesbury, as he became known on succeeding to the family earldom in 1851, was driven by solidly Christian convictions. Believing that God had sent His Son to Earth as a poor working man, Shaftesbury was convinced that no factory labourer should suffer more than strictly necessary in the appalling industrial climate of the day.

Shaftesbury's two greatest achievements were the passage of the Ten Hours Bill, which prevented factory owners from requiring their workforce to put in shifts of more than 10 hours' duration, and the establishment and support of numerous Ragged Schools which offered a basic education to the poor. He became greatly revered in the course of his life and when he died, aged 84, was interred in Westminster Abbey. The great philanthropist was commemorated, after his death, by the erection of a nude, winged statue in Piccadilly Circus. Titled by its sculptor *The Angel of Christian Charity*, it is today popularly known as *Eros*, its origin and true purpose utterly forgotten.

WILLIAM BOOTH
(1829–1912)
Founder of the Salvation Army

B orn near Nottingham eight years before Victoria's accession to the throne, William Booth's passionate commitment to the eradication of poverty was shaped by a tumultuous childhood.

Son of a builder whose early prosperity was followed by bankruptcy, Booth was forced to leave school and was apprenticed as a pawnbroker, a profession he detested. He spent much of his spare time organising Christian meetings, eventually becoming a Methodist lay preacher. In 1852, he became a full-time minister of the Wesleyan Church, but he was forced to quit his ministry when his superiors refused him permission to go outside his parish to preach. Booth instead founded a Christian Revival Society in the East End of London, which was aimed at bringing religion to the local poor, alcoholics and prostitutes.

In an effort to make the group more disciplined and effective, the Christian Revival Society was reorganised in the late 1870s along military lines and renamed the Salvation Army. Booth arranged for his 'soldiers' to be dressed in uniform and supplied with flags. Strongly believing in the power of music, he formed the Salvationists into brass bands and encouraged them to play the popular songs of the period, rewritten to feature religious lyrics.

As the leader of the Salvationists, Booth himself became widely known as 'General', and took his movement overseas, establishing the 'army' in a total of 58 countries by the time of his death in 1912.

Booth's work was heavily influenced by his wife, Catherine, an early feminist who had persuaded her husband that his view of women as 'the weaker sex' was unacceptable. Suitably impressed by her abilities as a preacher, Booth insisted that female members of the Salvation Army be seen as equals: 'My best men,' the general once remarked, 'are women.'

CHARLES BRADLAUGH
(1833–1891)
Militant atheist, urban radical

Charles Bradlaugh, the most notorious atheist of the Victorian period, grew up in a London working-class family. His background, one writer says, 'was that of a minor character in Dickens'. By profession, he was a soldier, purchasing his discharge from the army in 1853 and travelling to London to become a pamphleteer.

Adopting the pseudonym 'Iconoclast', Bradlaugh wrote a number of radical pamphlets and, by the 1860s, was generally recognised as one of the leading freethinkers in Britain. He helped to organise the National Secular Society, which opposed all Christian dogma, and published a radical journal named the *National Reformer*, which promoted secularism and women's rights.

Bradlaugh was renowned for his stubbornness, his beliefs spanned the entire range of what was considered dangerously revolutionary in Victorian times. He was a Republican, believed in universal suffrage, supported Home Rule for Ireland, and was a vigorous advocate of birth control. He was, however, bitterly opposed to socialism and was instead elected to parliament as Radical MP for Northampton in 1880.

Arriving at Westminster, Bradlaugh caused a scandal by refusing to take an oath of allegiance to the queen, and was several times forcibly prevented from taking his seat in the House of Commons. It was not until 1886 that the MP was permitted to affirm, rather than swear the oath of allegiance.

As an MP, Bradlaugh argued in favour of Republicanism and was a fierce opponent of public money being used to provide pensions for wealthy aristocratic servants of the state. An estimated 3,000 mourners, including Mohandas Gandhi, attended Bradlaugh's interment. In his will, the veteran agitator requested that 'my body be buried as cheaply as possible and no speeches be permitted at my funeral'.

THOMAS CARLYLE
(1795–1881)
Historian, puritan, hero-worshipper

Thomas Carlyle, born in Dumfriesshire, was a mathematics tutor and would-be astronomer who became the pre-eminent historian of Victorian Britain. His early years were not without their troubles. Carlyle's father was a rigid Calvinist, whose chief role in his son's life was to instil in him a fearsome work ethic. After graduating from Edinburgh University, he was forced to seek work as a private tutor, failed in his application to become a professor of astronomy, and lived in some poverty as a writer, thanks largely to his unwillingness to seek journalistic work. His early publications attracted little comment, and – having turned to the writing of history – he sent his friend John Stuart Mill the sole, handwritten copy of the first volume of his monumental *History of the French Revolution.* Unfortunately a maid unknowingly used the precious manuscript as kindling for the fire.

As a historian, Carlyle introduced an immediacy and a feel for action hitherto undreamed of. His works stressed the influence that individuals had over the course of events. His portrayal of a history determined by strong-minded heroes and villains (epitomised by the book *Heroes and Hero Worship*) proved influential in a Britain increasingly in thrall to the idea of empire. Later works attacked rampant capitalism and suggested that mercantile economies eroded communal values and spirituality.

A man of his time, Carlyle was an unapologetic defender of the superiority of the Anglo-Saxon and Germanic peoples, supported the institution of slavery, and organised a committee to defend the controversial Governor Eyre (see chapter III), who had violently quelled rebellion in Jamaica.

WILLIAM LOVETT
(1800–1877)
Peaceable Chartist and public librarian

A Cornishman and a cabinetmaker by trade, William Lovett gained renown as one of the leaders of the Chartists, a group regarded in the early Victorian period as dangerous revolutionaries for their insistence on such controversial reforms as universal suffrage, voting by secret ballot, and payment for members of parliament. Lovett was one of the authors of the eponymous Charter, drafted in May 1838 – his movement's call for political equality, social justice and parliamentary accountability. However, he clashed with the Chartists' more revolutionary wing, led by Feargus O'Connor, whose members were prepared to condone violence in the pursuit of their aims.

Thanks in part to O'Connor's blood and thunder speeches, the Chartists were regarded with fear and loathing by the country at large, and in 1839 Lovett was arrested and sentenced to a year in prison for describing the newly formed metropolitan police as 'a bloodthirsty and unconstitutional force'. A jury decided the comment amounted to seditious libel.

Lovett's spell in prison undermined his health, and he retired from active politics in 1842, devoting the remainder of his life to the cause of education for the working classes and promoting the establishment of circulating libraries. The bookshop he set up was not a commercial success, and he died, almost forgotten, in considerable poverty.

HENRY MANNING
(1808–1892)
Anglican turned Catholic cardinal, builder of Westminster Cathedral

Henry Manning, ordained an Anglican priest, was for many years one of the leading lights of the High Church wing of the Church of England. He converted to Catholicism in 1851 and advanced rapidly in the Roman Church, being appointed Archbishop of Westminster.

Manning's conversion to Catholicism came as the result of the ordination of a priest with views that Manning regarded as heresy. His abilities as a churchman already evident, he was welcomed into the Roman Catholic Church and demonstrated his considerable energy by founding a new church and congregation in Bayswater. When the See of Westminster fell vacant in 1865, Manning was appointed to it; three years later he secured the construction of a new cathedral. In his role as cardinal he became a close friend of Pope Leo XII. His influence on Catholic thinking was such that

Manning persuaded the pope to issue the *Rerum Novarum*, which stressed the Church's responsibility to fight for social justice. Manning was a noted campaigner on such issues, calling for the regeneration of London's East End and taking part in settling the London Dock Strike of 1889.

KARL MARX
(1818–1883)
German thinker and creator of Marxism

Karl Marx, the leading radical thinker of the 19th century, was born in Trier, Germany, lived in Paris and Brussels, but found sanctuary in Britain. It was while living in London and studying in the British Museum that Marx wrote the *Communist Manifesto* with Friedrich Engels, and the first volume of his critique of capitalism, *Das Kapital*. Marx was elected a member of the First International, which sought to spread the philosophy of Socialism, but earned a living as a foreign correspondent for *The New York Herald*.

During the 1850s, Marx and his aristocratic wife, Jenny, lived with their children in a cheap Soho apartment and were partially supported by Engels. Marx's writings were largely ignored during his life, and his last decade was marked by ill health, which limited his ability to work. He died aged 74 and was buried at Highgate Cemetery, his funeral attended by only 11 people.

CHARLES STEWART PARNELL
(1846–1891)
Member of parliament and 'uncrowned King of Ireland'

Handsome, aristocratic and utterly devoted to the interests of the country of his birth, Charles Stewart Parnell was a political giant of the 1880s. He held William Gladstone and his Liberal government in thrall with the threat of the withdrawal of Irish support in the House of Commons and almost secured his aim of Irish Home Rule. Born in County Wexford to a family of landowners, Parnell came to prominence in 1875 as a member of parliament for the Nationalist party. His abilities as an organiser and administrator were demonstrated in a thorough reorganisation of his party, which became a formidable and unified political machine under his leadership.

Parnell's spectacular political career was all but derailed in 1887 when *The Times* published letters showing that he had approved of, and apparently known in advance, the plan of a group of Fenian revolutionaries to murder two British government officials in Phoenix Park, Dublin. It was a particularly gruesome affair that had alarmed even committed advocates of Home Rule. The correspondence was, however, eventually shown to be a forgery, and his vindication made the MP a hero to a number of English Liberals.

Parnell's undoing was his messy private life, the public's attention being drawn to the long affair he had engaged in with a married woman, Kitty O'Shea, by whom he had three children. Kitty's divorce, and Parnell's determination to marry her, dented his popularity among Catholic voters.

The O'Shea scandal divided Parnell's party and he was forced to fight a bitter campaign to hold on to the leadership, during which he contracted pneumonia. Retiring temporarily to Brighton in search of a rest cure, Parnell died only a few days later, aged 45. He was, according to one lord, the most committed man seen in the House of Commons in a century and a half.

CHAPTER III

HEROES & IMPERIALISTS

JAMES BROOKE
(1803–1868)
'White rajah' of Sarawak

Most men of his era set their sights on becoming members of parliament, but not so James Brooke. This one-time Indian army officer not only established what amounted to a kingdom for himself in Sarawak, on the northern coast of Borneo, but also ruled over it as absolute monarch until his death in 1868.

Brooke arrived in Borneo by chance in 1838 and, using a £30,000 legacy from his father, helped the Sultan of Brunei suppress an uprising. He then pressed the reluctant sultan to reward his services by granting him suzerainty over Sarawak, a territory roughly the size of England. Sarawak was a largely unpromising place – covered in jungle and peopled by warring tribes – but Brooke was determined. He recruited a small military force, paid for from his inheritance, and largely suppressed the head-hunting and piracy endemic at the time.

Brooke never married or had children; it was rumoured that he had been shot through the genitals during service in Burma, but recent biographers have concluded that he was, in fact, homosexual. His nephew Charles succeeded him as rajah, and the Brooke family remained rulers of the territory until 1946.

SIR REDVERS BULLER
(1839–1908)
Soldier, Victoria Cross winner and scapegoat in the Boer War

Few of Queen Victoria's soldiers have so divided popular opinion as Sir Redvers Buller, an indubitably brave man whose career foundered on his poor handling of the Second Boer War.

Buller was born in Devonshire, the son of an MP, and joined the army in 1858. He won the Victoria Cross while serving in the Zulu Wars, where he rescued three companions from under the noses of the advancing impis, an exploit that gained him considerable renown. He participated in the First Boer War of 1881 and had reached the rank of general by the time the second South African conflict broke out in 1899. Despatched to Natal to resolve the situation, Buller found himself stymied by the Boers' superior numbers, weaponry and tactics, suffering a series of defeats that led to the nickname 'Reverse Buller'.

Hearing that he was to be replaced by Lord Roberts, Buller made one final attempt to win the war and launched an attack on a hill named Spion Kop. It ended in bloody defeat. Although initially acclaimed on his return to Britain, persistent criticism of the British army's performance in the war led the authorities to cast Buller as the scapegoat. He was retired on half pay, and his requests for a court martial – where he could plead his case – were refused.

ALEXANDER BURNES
(1805–1841)
Explorer, bestselling author, imperial martyr

Few men, even in the Victorian age, led lives of such excitement as that of Alexander Burnes. Born in Scotland and recruited to the East India Company, then overlord of much of India, Burnes arrived on the subcontinent at the age of 17. He proved to have a gift for languages, learning to speak Persian and Hindustani fluently. In 1831 he was chosen to lead a mission to take a gift of horses to Ranjit Singh, the great Sikh leader – an exercise he used as a chance to spy on Sikh territory. This adventure gave Burnes a taste for exploration and espionage and, with the help of a loyal Kashmiri named Mohan Lal, he spent the next few years travelling in several little-known areas of the East.

The book that Burnes published on his eventual return to London became a bestseller and sparked considerable interest in Asia, which offered a potential route for a Russian attack on India. As a consequence, Burnes became heavily involved in the intrigues that led the East India Company to place a puppet ruler named Shah Shuja on the throne of Afghanistan. Burnes, who had argued forcefully that Shah Shuja was too unpopular to last for long in such an unstable kingdom, was sent to Kabul as part of the British delegation and, in 1841, became the victim of a furious mob rioting in support of a rival candidate known as Dost Mohammed. The revolt led to the disaster of the First Afghan War, which saw all but one member of the British garrison in Afghanistan killed.

It was said that, when it became clear that death was inevitable, Burnes left the protection of his house and advanced on the crowd, a black cloth tied over his eyes so that he could not see the blows that would kill him. Seconds later, he was cut to pieces by the furious mob.

GEORGE CURZON
(1859–1925)
Youthful viceroy of India whose vast potential went unfulfilled

A mong the ranks of Victorian imperialists, George Curzon stands out as having had the most potential for greatness. A brilliant student at Eton and Oxford, he was elected to parliament at 26 and soon became Under-Secretary of State for India. In 1899, at only 39, he was named Viceroy of India – the youngest in history. He was elevated to the peerage so as to convey the necessary sense of prestige to the princes of the subcontinent.

Curzon served in India for six years, restored the Taj Mahal and played a vigorous part in the 'Great Game' – the eternal struggle in High Asia between representatives of the Russian and British governments. He formed a passionate hatred for Horatio Kitchener who was in India to reform the Indian army. In later life, Curzon returned to the UK, joined the Conservative party, and was named foreign secretary soon after World War I. He never became prime minister, and in the opinion of

Winston Churchill, failed to achieve his potential: 'The morning had
been golden; the noontide was bronze; and the evening lead. But all were
polished 'til it shone after its fashion.'

EDWARD JOHN EYRE
(1815–1901)
Explorer, colonial governor and reviled imperialist

Tall, thin, pigeon-chested and bearded, Edward John Eyre left England
for Australia at the tender age of 17, sailing there alone to explore the
Southern Australian wilderness with an Aboriginal companion, Wylie.

He came to public attention in 1841, when he undertook a journey of
unbelievable harshness and almost total pointlessness along the Great
Australian Bight between Adelaide and Albany. Eyre was the first white
man to survive the trek across the waterless Nullabor Plain, which was only
possible due to the relations he kept with local tribes who showed him how
to extract water from sand dunes and tree roots. Although no discoveries
resulted from the trip, it made Eyre a hero in Australia, where Lake Eyre is
named after him.

However, Eyre's privations may have altered his character for the worst,
as his subsequent posting, as lieutenant governor of New Zealand, was
marked by displays of peevishness and an increasing obsession with gold
braid. In 1862 he was transferred to the Caribbean, becoming governor of
Jamaica, an island that had never recovered from the emancipation of its
slaves several decades earlier and which was rife with rumours of uprisings.
The expected rebellion occurred in 1865, when a group of militant Baptists
from an isolated village known as Stony Gut appeared in the nearest town
and massacred 17 of its white inhabitants. Eyre reacted vigorously, sending
in troops to suppress the rebellion and arresting not only its leader, but also
George William Gordon, the chief critic of the British government on the
island. Eyre's decisive action ended the rebellion and made him a hero to

white planters, but he was criticised at home. Recalled to England, he was threatened with indictment but never actually prosecuted. He retreated to an anonymous life in rural Somerset where he died some 30 years later.

JACKY FISHER
(1841–1920)
Extraordinary admiral, fierce reformer

The Battle of Trafalgar (1804) assured Britain of command of the sea for a century, but was not entirely good news for the all-powerful Royal Navy. Deprived of any realistic chance of fighting a major war, the service became arrogant and apathetic. By 1884, the situation had degenerated to such a point that there was considerable public controversy concerning its ability to fight at all. Enter Jacky Fisher, unarguably the most outstanding admiral since Nelson, a vivacious man whose enthusiasm – not to mention his ability to hold a grudge – was to mark the navy, for better or worse, for generations.

Born in Ceylon, Fisher's skin took on a curious yellow tint that led his many enemies to dub him 'The Asiatic', with all the cunning that implied. Fisher, like most of his contemporaries, saw little action during his career, but proved to be a formidable administrator. He revolutionised the teaching of gunnery at *HMS Excellent* and torpedo warfare at *HMS Vernon.* He went to the admiralty as controller of the navy in 1892, in charge of ship design and procurement. He demanded and received the best from his crews, working the men furiously to improve their efficiency.

In person, Fisher attracted and repelled in equal measure. Favourites were promoted and showered with desirable appointments; enemies reviled and 'cast into the outer darkness'. Much given to writing excitable letters littered with exclamation marks and closures such as 'Yours till charcoal sprouts!', Fisher was also a notorious flirt. Although he apparently remained physically faithful to his wife of more than 50 years, he ended his days living with an adoring, if conveniently married, duchess.

By the time of Queen Victoria's death, Fisher was on the cusp of greatness: commander-in-chief of the Mediterranean fleet (Britain's largest) and in line to be nominated as first sea lord – the professional head of the navy. In the course of the next eight challenging years, he would tear his service apart and rebuild it, introducing all big gun battleships and submarines, withdrawing useless squadrons from distant waters, and readying the fleet for action in World War I. Recalled briefly to service during that conflict, he died in 1920.

CHARLES GORDON
(1833–1885)
Soldier and old China hand

For a member of the Royal Engineers – traditionally the most stolid and least imaginative of British army regiments – Charles Gordon was a considerable anomaly. Able and conscientious, he was also prone to mysticism and was thoroughly distrustful of earthly passions. 'I wished,' he wrote, 'I was a eunuch at 14… All that the flesh admires is doomed. Cursed is the man who makes flesh his aim.'

Gordon served in the Crimean War, distinguishing himself with several acts of reckless bravery, and in the early 1860s found himself in China, where he fought in the Opium Wars, personally supervising the burning of the Summer Palace outside Beijing. Soon afterwards, a vast rebellion led by a quasi-Christian group known as the Taipings, broke out. Gordon was seconded to the Chinese army to help put down the rebellion, and trained a force that, due to its numerous successes, became known as the Ever-Victorious army. Gordon returned to Britain a hero, and was known thereafter as 'Chinese' Gordon.

The next five years were spent in command of the Royal Engineers detachment at Gravesend, where Gordon developed his own mystical brand of Christianity. This faith marked him out when he was sent to serve in the British Protectorate of Egypt to assist the Egyptian army in extending the country's power south of the border with Abyssinia (now Ethiopia). He also displayed increasing signs of a death wish, writing: 'I do not want to hang on. How I wish He would come.'

During his second tour of duty in the Sudan, Gordon occupied the capital, Khartoum, and held it against a revolutionary Muslim army led by a religious figure known as the Mahdi. He refused several chances to be evacuated from the city – biographers have speculated that he actively wished to become a Christian martyr. He was speared to death when, in January 1885, the Mahdi's forces broke into the city and massacred the remnants of his force.

HORATIO KITCHENER
(1850–1916)
General, animal lover, recruitment poster icon

Cold and autocratic even by the standards of the British army, Horatio Kitchener was also one of the most able soldiers of his day, earning a reputation for rescuing situations rendered all but untenable by incompetent fellow officers. His greatest triumph was to avenge the death of Charles Gordon at Khartoum. Kitchener, in command of the Egyptian army, marched south and massacred the Mahdi's troops at the Battle of Omdurman in 1898, a victory achieved largely thanks to the employment of machine guns.

Two years later, the then General Kitchener was sent to South Africa and placed in command of British forces struggling to subdue the Boers. His methods – which included herding women and children into unsanitary 'concentration camps' – were brutal but effective, and the British forces won.

Kitchener's private life was the subject of gossip, then and now. In at least one country house, younger members of the household were known to ask their servants to sleep across the doorways to their bedrooms when he came to stay in the hope of averting unwanted visits in the dead of night. Though all but devoid of human warmth, Kitchener doted on animals, forming close attachments with the horses and camels that carried him on his campaigns, and kept a pack of four cocker spaniels named Shot, Bang, Miss and Damn.

Kitchener was made a field marshal in 1909 and elevated to an earldom five years later. On the outbreak of war in 1914 he was asked to join the Cabinet as secretary of state for war, and it was his face and jabbing finger that appeared on a memorable recruitment poster urging Britain's youth that 'Kitchener wants YOU. Join your country's army.'

Kitchener died in 1916 while en route to Russia, when the ship on which he was travelling struck a mine and sank. His death by drowning, it is said, had been predicted to him 22 years earlier by Cheiro, the noted society palm reader.

CHARLES NAPIER
(1782–1853)
General and investigator of the homosexual brothels of Karachi

Charles Napier – arrogant, prickly, compulsively sarcastic and almost the last in a long line of Scottish imperialists – was an outstanding figure of the early Victorian period, in both senses of the word. Professionally, he was a talented soldier, and victor in one of the most celebrated campaigns of the age. Physically, he was possessed of a hook nose and glaring eyes, and habitually dressed in an idiosyncratic uniform consisting of spectacles, corduroy breeches and unusual helmets, all of his own design.

Those who penetrated the general's ferocious exterior discovered that a kindly and deeply inquisitive man lay beneath. It was Napier who commissioned the young Richard Burton to investigate the homosexual brothels of Karachi because, as Burton wrote, he had 'a curiosity about their workings'.

Although of aristocratic stock, Napier was far from rich, had been educated at an ordinary village school, and lived between assignments in considerable poverty. On one occasion, summoned by the government to take the post of commander of an entire division of the Indian army, he was found living over a butcher's shop in Nottingham with less than £2 to his name.

Napier's military career began at the age of 11, but after being severely wounded fighting against Napoleon in the Peninsular campaign, he did not command an army in the field until he was 60. He made the most of the opportunity, however; when assigned the task of subduing the province of Sindh, in what is now Pakistan, he crushed all opposition, took £60,000 in prize money and set himself up as ruler of the territory at a salary of £15,000 a year. Word of this famous victory led *Punch* to jest that Napier had announced his conquest in a single-word despatch to headquarters: *peccavi*, Latin for 'I have sinned'.

The general's own philosophy of imperial government was typically concise; newly conquered peoples, he believed, should be subjected to 'a good thrashing first, and great kindness afterwards'.

CECIL RHODES
(1853–1902)
Father of the British empire in southern Africa

No man was a more fervent believer in the British empire than Cecil Rhodes. A vicar's son from Bishop's Stortford who made a fortune from the Kimberley gold fields, he rose to become the most powerful man in Africa. Rhodes emigrated to South Africa in 1870 in the hope of restoring his fragile health and successfully invested his money in the territory's then depressed diamond mines. Wealth allowed him to embark upon a political career that reached its apogee with his elevation to the position of premier of the Cape Colony, in what is now South Africa. He planned a 'Cape-to-Cairo' railway to link Britain's colonies in Africa. He also urged his own British South Africa Company to annex large swathes of what is now Zambia and Zimbabwe. These districts became the British territory of Rhodesia, named in his honour.

Rhodes was proud of both his and his country's achievements. He said: 'I contend that we are the finest race in the world; and that the more of the world we inhabit, the better it is for the human race.' His determination to make the whole of South Africa a British colony led him to back the notorious Jameson Raid into the Boer territories inland, which helped to spark the Boer War.

Rhodes' calling was to attend to the self-imposed duty of the great Anglo-Saxon nations to assume what Kipling called 'the White Man's Burden'. To this end he endowed a number of Rhodes Scholarships, enabling American students to study at Oxford University, which are still awarded today. Much of the rest of his wealth was allocated in his will to the foundation of a secret society which had as its avowed intention the extension of British rule across the world and the reintegration of the United States into the empire.

ARTHUR WELLESLEY,
1ST DUKE OF WELLINGTON
(1769–1852)
Military hero, prime minister, master of the pithy quote

For a man described by his own mother as 'food for powder, and no more', Arthur Wellesley, the immortal Duke of Wellington, did well for himself. Removed from Eton and sent to a French military academy by a family that despaired of his negligible academic abilities, Wellington honed his military skills on Indian battlefields. He later went on to face Napoleon and won victories in Portugal, Spain and at Waterloo. The prestige and awards of money by a grateful parliament sustained him through nearly four more decades of public life. He spent the 1820s and 1830s as a government minister, commander-in-chief of the British army, and from 1828 to 1830 was prime minister, fighting to prevent the disintegration of the Tory party over the issues of economic reform and Catholic emancipation. He served Robert Peel as foreign secretary in the 1830s and was leader of the House of Lords in the Tory government of 1841–1846.

Wellington made a far from popular prime minister, being reactionary and fearing reform would lead to revolution. Today, his public service is often seen as selfless in a period in which self-interest and patronage dominated politics. He refused to oppose every measure put forward by the Whigs, saying: 'A factious opposition is highly injurious to the interests of the country.'

Wellington was surprisingly slight, and his beaky nose earned him the nickname 'Old Hookey'. His marriage was not happy, and he occasionally availed himself of the services of courtesans. During the 1820s one such woman, the notorious Harriette Wilson, wrote to some 200 of her richest clients demanding a payment of £200, or £20 a year, to keep their names out of her memoirs; Wellington's supposed response was 'Publish and be damned!' He went on to feature prominently in Wilson's book. He died aged 83 and was awarded the last heraldic state funeral in Britain.

GARNET WOLSELEY
(1833–1913)
Field marshal and reformer who became a byword for efficiency

In his day, Sir Garnet Wolseley was renowned as the most capable of all British officers. He secured victory in a string of brilliant campaigns, including the suppression of the Metis (French-Indian trappers in the Canadian wilderness) in 1870, the superbly executed Ashanti War of 1873–1874 and the Zululand campaign of 1879–1880.

Suitably distressed by the incompetence that he saw in the army, Wolseley devoted much of the remainder of his career to searching for the cleverest young officers, many of whom he recruited to the 'Wolseley Ring', a group of reformers who played a very significant role in modernising the country's military forces. Wolseley received the honour of being named commander-in-chief of the British army in 1895. During the late Victorian period, Wolseley's reputation for efficiency was so great that his name became synonymous with smooth-running efficiency, as in, things are 'all Sir Garnet'.

CHAPTER IV

✤

ECCENTRIC SOULS

FRANCIS TREVELYAN BUCKLAND
(1826–1880)
Zoophagen with extreme eating habits

British palates may be becoming more adventurous with every passing year, but few can match the experiences of Francis Trevelyan Buckland, the naturalist, writer and 'experimental zoophagen' who supped on whale ('too strong, even when boiled with charcoal'), rhinoceros (baked into pies for his lecture audiences), and elephant trunk (brewed into a 'rubbery' soup). He also organised the Eland Dinner in 1859, at which he attempted to open a wider debate about the nature of Victorian food with a discussion about whether or not eland (an African antelope with spiral horns) should be introduced into the national diet.

As a boy, Buckland was said to have fried mice, garden snails, frogs and hedgehogs in batter and even declared that roast field mouse was a 'splendid *bonne bouché* for a hungry boy'. While a student, he exhumed a panther that had been buried at the Surrey Zoological Gardens for two days. He proceeded to devour the carcass, pronouncing it 'not very good'.

By the time he reached Oxford University, Buckland was plainly eccentric by today's standards, although he was a hard-working naturalist according to the rather different mores of the Victorian era. He kept a menagerie that variously included a jackal, a bear called Tilglath-Pileser, a chameleon, some marmots and an eagle. The bear was 'mesmerised' by Lord Houghton at the Oxford meeting of the British Association in 1847.

Once out in the world, Buckland proved no less controversial, although his public – piqued by his four-volume *Curiosities of Natural History* – loved to hear outlandish stories about him. He was reported to have bottle-fed a dolphin in a railway carriage. He carried a matchbox full of little toads the size of beans in his pocket. He marched down Albany Street in London arm-in-arm with a dwarf and a giant. He kept an oven-ready dead hippopotamus at the bottom of the stairs in his home. But most controversially of all, he incensed the priests of the shrine of St Rosalia in Palermo by denouncing the saint's relics as 'the bones of a goat'.

Undaunted by the unpopular reaction to eland, Buckland set up the Acclimatisation Society in 1860 to further the search for new food. At meetings some 100 guests were served exotic dishes, such as bird's nest soup, tripang (Japanese sea slug) and soup made from sinews of axis deer.

One consequence of Buckland's efforts was that, for the next decade, several gentry began speculative stock raising. Lord Breadalbane gamely raised yaks and American bison on his Taymouth estate, Lord Bute stocked his Scottish islands with beavers and many people were even persuaded to raise kangaroos.

RICHARD BURTON
(1821–1890)
Explorer, Arabist and translator of the unexpurgated Arabian Nights

Richard Burton left Trinity College, Oxford degree-less and in disgrace. He departed tooting on a tin trumpet as he drove a dogcart over the sacred flower-beds, but he was also a clever linguist, master of 25 languages.

With a desire for adventure, Burton's first commission, to penetrate the boy brothels of Karachi for the Indian army with a view to stamping out these 'unspeakable haunts of the Persian vice', was a disaster. 'Ruffian Dick, the White Nigger', as his fellow officers knew him, painted far too intimate a picture of these dens, and so Burton was swiftly and quietly sidelined.

Thus repudiated for a second time by the hated establishment, Burton began a life of travel, adventure and writing. Many of his missions entailed disguise and the use of skills acquired in the Indian army.

His travels took him first to Goa and Sindh, then on to Arabia, where he penned the book that made him famous, *Pilgrimage to El Medinah and Mecca*. He moved on to the forbidden city of Harar in Abyssinia and from there undertook an arduous trek to find the source of the Nile. After this adventure, with typical unpredictability, he journeyed to Utah and Salt Lake City, where he explored the cult world of Mormonism, disguised as an elder.

Thought to be bisexual, Burton married an adoring woman, Isobel, who networked, charmed and wheedled many expatriates on his behalf, eventually winning a slot for him in the consular service. Posted off to Fernando Po, he laboured away on his own, until eventually he could transfer to Brazil, where Isobel joined him. A romantic but brief posting to Damascus was followed by a long twilight in Trieste (some 18 years) as the almost ludicrously under-worked consul.

But Burton's literary output never ceased and the quantity of work he produced was phenomenal. He translated *The Book of a Thousand Nights and One Night* – better known as *The Arabian Nights* – in 16 volumes, and *The Kama Sutra*. He also wrote works on travel, swords, vampires, cannibals, Jews, farting (sadly lost) and even scalping. 'Scalps come off,' he wrote, 'with a sound which, I am told, is not unlike a "flop".'

When 'Gypsy Dick' died in 1890, his wife laid him to rest in a marble tent in Surrey, designed to represent a Bedouin tent with its implicit resonance of romance and adventure.

WILLIAM CAVENDISH-SCOTT-BENTINCK
(1800–1879)
Duke, eccentric, alleged proprietor of London's largest furniture bazaar

The British aristocracy, it has to be said, has produced more than its share of outlandish characters, but few have been quite as eccentric as William Cavendish-Scott-Bentinck, the 5th Duke of Portland.

The first few decades of the duke's life passed free of incident, but after his stumbling proposal to the actress Adelaide Kemble was summarily rejected, Bentinck retired from public life. He preferred thereafter to remain unacknowledged even by the substantial number of staff at his ancestral home at Welbeck Abbey. Servants who chanced upon the duke were under orders to pass him 'as they would a tree'; those who failed to obey this dictum were made to roller-skate on Bentinck's private rink 'until exhausted'.

The duke eventually retreated to a small suite of rooms within the abbey, abandoning the rest of the structure to ruin. He took his meals and gave orders through a pair of letterboxes (one for incoming material, the other for outgoing). Much of the family fortune was expended on vast excavations beneath the abbey. Although Bentinck received no visitors, he built the largest private ballroom in the country below ground, and excavated a two-kilometre-long tunnel leading to the nearest railway station. When journeying up to London, Bentinck would board a special windowless carriage, drive it unseen through his tunnel, and have it placed directly on the train. Servants in his London home were never completely sure he was on board until well after his arrival.

A genuinely kindly man, the duke provided each servant with his own donkey and umbrella. In the latter part of his life he ate little but roast chicken, delivered to him on a miniature railway running through the underground tunnels. After his death, his heir discovered that each of the rooms his relative had occupied at Welbeck had been painted pink and that each, even the dining room, had had a lavatory installed. Several cupboards held nothing but boxes of brown wigs. Even after his death the duke's legacy continued to raise eyebrows. In 1896, a woman named Anna Druce went to court to claim that the reclusive Bentinck had actually spent more than 20 years of his life working incognito, as Thomas Druce (owner of the Baker Street Furniture Bazaar) and that she, as his daughter-in-law, was heir to the family fortune. It was only with the exhumation of Druce's corpse that the matter was finally resolved in 1907.

DANIEL DUNGLAS HOME
(1833–1886)
Medium of choice to the rich and famous

Despite a growing tide of scepticism against all manifestations of the supernatural as Victoria's reign progressed, celebrity medium Daniel Dunglas Home enjoyed continued admiration, with figures such as Bulwer

Lytton, John Ruskin, William Makepeace Thackeray, Henry Wadsworth Longfellow and Ralph Waldo Emerson claiming he was 'a prodigious genius'.

Originally born in Edinburgh, the medium was adopted by an American aunt and soon discovered that he had 'second sight'. He returned to Britain in 1855, claiming an unproven descent from the 10th Earl of Home. He subsisted off the bounty of others, considering that his mission in life was to prove the existence of immortality, which would 'draw us nearer to God'. He influenced a Mrs Jane Lyons to adopt him as a son and give him £33,000 as a gift. She later retracted her promise and sued him.

As a medium, Home's performances went far beyond traditional spirit 'hands' and raps. He once levitated out of one window of a house only to return via another, allegedly floated above the heads of audiences, and projected tongues of fire from his head. In the 'tongues of fire' display, Home dazzled his audience with a display of incomprehensible gabble, explaining that the performance was a repeat of the first Pentecost, when the Holy Spirit had entered the Apostles in the same manner.

JOHN KIRKHAM
(c. 1830–1876)
Steward-turned-Ethiopian general

The story of hapless John Kirkham, a Devonian hotelier, adventurer and ship's steward, provides a salutary lesson of the dangers of displeasing Queen Victoria.

Kirkham fought with General Charles Gordon in the Taiping Rebellion, where he was twice wounded in the head. This seems to have caused a personality imbalance. Arriving in Ethiopia as a ship's steward with the P&O line, just as the British army was preparing to invade, he saw an opportunity to enter the fray as a military provisions expert. Following the end of the campaign against Emperor Tewodos in 1868, Kirkham advised the incoming Emperor Yohannes IV to create a Western-style 'disciplined force' which crushed the emperor's rival, Wagshum Gobeze, in the 1871 invasion of Tigray. After another success at the Battle of Asum on 11 July, Kirkham was promoted to the rank of general and sent to Europe as an imperial Abyssinian ambassador. He visited London, and also possibly Paris, before returning to Massawa in February 1873.

Kirkham's 15 minutes of fame were now rapidly drawing to a close. In December 1875, he was captured attempting to cross Egyptian lines to reach Europe and imprisoned in a large lion's cage. His captors gave him little or no food but, instead, supplied copious amounts of alcohol to drink in the hope that he would 'be compelled to feed upon the insects on his body'. When he was finally discovered ragged, half-naked, and starving by a party of British sailors from *HMS Teazer*, a cablegram from London informed them he had sacrificed the right to British protection. They left him there.

Kirkham died six months later of alcoholism and dysentery at the Lutheran mission in Massawa.

JOSEPH MERRICK
(1862–1890)
The Elephant Man

Born in Leicester to Mary Jane Merrick, Joseph Merrick began to exhibit deformity from either the age of two or of five, depending on which source is to be believed.

When he was 11, his crippled mother died and he was forced to live with his father, Joseph Rockley Merrick, and his stepmother, who disliked his presence. Forced out on to the streets to sell shoe polish, where children would continually harass him, Merrick made a living as a sideshow attraction, eventually travelling to Belgium in 1886 where he was mistreated and abandoned by a showman. After making his way back to London, Merrick was rescued by Dr Frederick Treves, who found him curled up in the corner of a train station suffering from a severe bronchial infection. Dr Treves, acting both professionally and out of curiosity, took him for treatment at the London Hospital. He was eventually offered a permanent home there.

Once installed in the hospital, Merrick became, to a certain extent, a darling of society, even to the point of becoming a favourite of Queen Victoria. Although he was happy living at the London Hospital, Merrick often commented that he would like to transfer to a hospital for the blind in the hope of finding a woman who would not be repulsed by his appearance.

In later years, Merrick found solace in writing prose and poetry. He died on 11 April 1890 after an apparently accidental suffocation. It seems he had abandoned his usual foetal sleeping position and lain on his back, in an attempt to imitate 'normal' sleeping posture, and had consequently suffocated due to the heaviness of his head.

LIEUTENANT-GENERAL AUGUSTUS HENRY LANE FOX PITT RIVERS
(1827–1900)
Anthropologist and museum founder

Very few people can fail to be inspired by the Gothic splendour and magnificence of the Pitt Rivers Museum in Oxford. It was founded in 1884 by Lieutenant-General Augustus Henry Lane Fox Pitt Rivers, an influential figure in the development of archaeology and evolutionary anthropology.

From its immense Gothic windows to its soaring glass and metal interior, the whole building is a monument to adventure. It was built to house the founding gift of 18,000 anthropological objects from Pitt Rivers, which has now increased to over half a million objects. But what of Pitt Rivers himself, without whom this eclectic collection of textiles, sculpture, masks, skins, magic amulets and much more wouldn't exist?

Pitt Rivers was a solitary man who left few traces, yet we know that he was born in Yorkshire to a wealthy landowning family. After graduating from Sandhurst, he served in the Crimean War, transferring to Malta to train soldiers in the use of the new Minié rifle, before being promoted to lieutenant-colonel, and finally returning to England.

In 1861, Pitt Rivers was sent to eastern Canada following the *Trent* incident which occurred during the American Civil War. The arrival of British troops soon saw the Confederate representatives who had been seized from the *Trent* steamer released. Pitt Rivers used his time there to collect artefacts. He finally retired from army life in 1882 at the age of 55, and enjoyed a long and fruitful period of retirement pursuing his interests.

SAMUEL SCOTT
(b. unknown, d. 1841)
Exhibitionist, diver and hanged man

Samuel Gilbert Scott, who was born and raised in Philadelphia and known professionally as 'The American Diver', was an expert at holding his breath and exhibited incredible muscular control.

Famed for a dive off a ledge just below Niagara Falls (estimated as 593 feet above the surface of the water), Scott arrived in England in 1840. There he leapt from a 200-foot topmast on the battleship *St Joseph* at Devonport and, perhaps most alarmingly, from a 240-foot cliff at Cornwall into only eight feet of water.

Scott survived at least one serious accident before his final demise. After one performance on an American ship at Deptford, consisting of swinging from his feet and neck in a ship's rigging, he slipped while positioning the noose he employed to add an element of danger to the act and turned black in the face. In a desperate attempt to save himself, Scott flung his feet upward and they were caught, almost miraculously, by a sailor who supported his body until he could free himself.

Silly money was offered for his next stunt, and on 11 January 1841, Scott 'challenged the world for 100 guineas'. He would run, he said, from the White Lion Pub in Drury Lane to Waterloo Bridge, jump 40 feet into the river, and return, all within the hour. In the midst of his pre-dive display on the bridge, Scott's noose suddenly tightened and he remained suspended over the Thames for several minutes while the crowd applauded wildly, thinking that this was part of the act. In fact, The American Diver was dead.

CHARLES DE LAET WALDO SIBTHORP
(1783–1855)
Extremist Tory

K nown as 'Colonel Sibthorp', Charles de Laet Waldo Sibthorp was a widely caricatured British Tory politician in the early 19th century. Following in the footsteps of his father, his brother and his great-uncle, he sat as MP for Lincoln from 1826 to 1855 (with one brief break) as well as becoming a colonel in the South Lincolnshire Militia. He can best be described as an ultra-Tory eccentric in white nankeen trousers, large white hat and top boots, thundering against every innovation, from railways to the Prince Consort's allowance.

Sibthorp was born into a gentrified Lincolnshire family. He fought in the Napoleonic Wars and continued in the service until 1822, when he succeeded to the family estates, marrying Maria Tottenham in 1812 with whom he had four children.

During the three decades that Sibthorp spent in parliament, he became known as one of its most reactionary members. He opposed just about everything, from Catholic to Jewish emancipation; the repeal of the Corn Laws to the Reform Act of 1832; and the Great Exhibition of 1851. Sibthorp died at his home in London and was succeeded as MP by his son, Gervaise.

THE FEMALE BLONDIN/SELINA WILD (MLLE VIOLANTE)
(*fl.* 1862)
Tightrope artist and tribute act

In 1862, tightrope walker Blondin followed up his walk across Niagara Falls with feats of derring-do at the Crystal Palace, where he crossed the Centre Transept 55 metres above the ground while pushing his five-year-old daughter in a wheelbarrow.

Just one year earlier, a woman called Selina Wild, dubbing herself 'The Female Blondin', had paid tribute to him by attempting to cross the River Thames – an attempt which failed spectacularly.

An enormous crowd of 100,000 people allegedly watched Miss Wild, whose real name was Mlle Pauline Violante, as she teetered onto the wire at Battersea and set off. To her credit, she almost made it, getting four fifths of the way across the river before she supposedly discovered that some of the guy ropes that held the wire steady had been cut loose, forcing her to be lowered into a boat.

With immense gusto, Wild made a second attempt, this time successful, which was described as 'made in the light of the declining sun, her gold-broidered dress and white pole gleaming refulgently'.

DAVID WILKIE WINFIELD
(1837–1887)
Painter of Elizabethan pastiches and leader of the St John's Wood Clique

Victorian England was a fusion of materialism and references to the past. The painter David Wilkie Winfield, later Wynfield, was a typical creature of this age, referencing all things poetic and 'ancient', and even dressing up in Elizabethan costumes.

Born in India, his training began at 'Dagger' Leigh's studio in Newman Street, where he painted historical subjects, such as Oliver Cromwell and the

Duke of Buckingham. In the 1860s, Winfield and his friends became known as the 'St John's Wood Clique', a group of self-consciously dandyish and bohemian young men who enjoyed being photographed in fancy dress. They took this enjoyment to the extreme; whether they were donning Elizabethan ruffs, breastplates or turbans for the camera, no pose proved too extreme or coy.

Although Winfield was known at the time as a successful painter who exhibited at the Royal Academy, today he is best remembered for his soft-focus photographic portraits of more famous artists, including Edouard Manet, John Millais, Lord Frederic and Edward Burne-Jones, taken in the 1860s.

CHAPTER V

PIONEERS OF
PROGRESS

JOSEPH BAZALGETTE
(1819–1891)
Engineer who tackled the 'Great Stink of London'

As late as the middle of the 19th century, London's sewer system was still medieval in design and construction. Many houses discharged their waste into the city's 200,000 overflowing cesspits; a limited and crumbling network of underground sewers spewed its contents, untreated, directly into the River Thames. Waterborne disease, notably cholera, was rife and the river itself was dead, unable to support marine life in the vicinity of London. Anyone unfortunate enough to fall into the Thames and swallow a mouthful of its waters was quite likely to die.

The cost and difficulty of engineering a solution to the sewer system's problems prevented modernisation until the very hot summer of 1858, when the sweltering sewage polluting the river became so noxious that it interfered with the running of the Houses of Parliament. By August, emergency legislation had been passed allowing £3 million to be spent on sewage works.

The man given the task of ensuring that the 'Great Stink of London' was never repeated was Joseph Bazalgette, the son of a naval officer and, by trade, a railway engineer. Bazalgette conceived an enormous new system of tunnels that were designed to run along the banks of the Thames and intercept existing sewers before they could disgorge their contents. One consequence of Bazalgette's plan was the construction of the Victoria, Albert and Chelsea embankments, built to house the much-needed new system of sewers.

Bazalgette's great project took well over a decade to complete. Even then, it merely discharged the same untreated sewage into the Thames east of London, and it wasn't until the end of the century that treatment plants were built at the outfalls in Becton and Crossness. But its worth, to the health of Londoners, was recognised with a knighthood bestowed on Bazalgette in 1874.

Today, the only public memorial to Bazalgette's achievement is a small bust hidden beneath a railway bridge at Charing Cross. His real monument, though, was the most useful public work constructed in London in the 19th century. It was a masterpiece of engineering of which *The Times*

commented, in his obituary: 'Of the great sewer that runs beneath
Londoners, as a rule, know nothing, though the Registrar-General could tell
them that its existence has added some 20 years to their chance of life.'

ALEXANDER GRAHAM BELL
(1847–1922)
Inventor of the telephone and holder of the world's most valuable patent

A Scot born in Edinburgh, who became a naturalised American, Alexander
Graham Bell was born into a family devoted to the teaching of the deaf,
and turned his lifelong interest in communication into a revolutionary device
that made him one of the richest inventors of the century.

Bell's first job was as a teacher of elocution in Elgin, and it was not until
shortly before he emigrated with his family to Canada, at the age of 23, that he
began to display an interest in the science of telephony. The basic principles
required to transmit sound by the means of vibration were already known
at the time, and had been employed by several inventors. But no technique
capable of making human speech intelligible at a distance existed until Bell
filed Patent 174,465 for a 'method of, and apparatus for, transmitting vocal or
other sounds telegraphically' with the US Patent Office in 1876.

The newfangled telephone created an immediate sensation and within a
decade it was revolutionising business and communications. Bell continued
to develop the technology and was awarded a further 17 patents, but it was
his first, which gave him an effective monopoly over the invention everybody
wanted to use, that made him an immensely wealthy man.

In later life, the inventor's new interests saw him developing the hydrofoil
and the aeroplane. He and his laboratory assistants were also the first to
conceive of recording information using magnetic fields, a technology that
subsequently led to cassette tapes and floppy disks.

History records the first-ever phone call as that between Bell and his
assistant, Thomas Watson, after the inventor accidentally spilt acid down

his trousers. According to tradition, the message conveyed in this first emergency call was: 'Mr Watson, come here, I need you.' Several writers, including J Edward Hyde, author of *The Telephone Book*, have speculated that this original call may actually have been somewhat less dignified.

❧

ISAMBARD KINGDOM BRUNEL
(1806–1859)
Engineering genius, builder of bridges, railways and ships

Isambard Kingdom Brunel, arguably the most outstanding engineer of the 19th century, remains an icon today. The image of the great engineer standing in front of his ship, the *Great Eastern*, wearing a stovepipe hat, cigar clenched firmly between his teeth and fingers thrust assertively into his jacket, epitomises the self-confidence and ability of this Victorian engineer.

Brunel learnt his trade on his father Marc's great triumph, the Thames Tunnel, meticulously constructed through the saturated mud of east London. Brunel built the Clifton Suspension Bridge (not completed until 1864), the Great Western Railway between 1833 and 1841 and its Box Tunnel (then the longest in the world), and the *Great Western*, the first steamship to cross the Atlantic (launched in 1837).

Almost everything that Brunel did was bigger, faster and better than that which had gone before. The *Great Western* more than halved the time required for a crossing from Bristol to New York. The *Great Britain*, his second ship, launched in 1843 and was the first ocean-going propeller-driven ship, and the *Great Eastern*, his third, was – at 700 feet – six times the size of any iron predecessor: so huge, in fact, that it took 200 men working for two years to break her up.

Suffering considerably in later life from kidney stones, Brunel died of a stroke, aged only 53, but left his country with an unparalleled legacy, as many of the bridges and tunnels that he built are still in use today.

CHARLES DARWIN
(1809–1882)
Co-discoverer of the principles of evolution

Charles Darwin, perhaps more than any other figure of the 19th century, is remembered for a single brilliant idea: the principle of natural selection. But the discovery wasn't the by-product of a moment of genius. Biology was the fourth subject Darwin had taken up (he had rebelled at attempts to teach him classics and medicine, and eventually went to Cambridge to read theology), and he spent two decades mulling over the details of his theory before finally publishing it. Even then, it only went to print when he realised that another scientist, Alfred Russell Wallace, had independently reached similar conclusions.

A grandson of both Erasmus Darwin, a noted scientist, and Josiah Wedgwood, the great potter, whose fortune freed him to devote his life to study, Darwin was brought up in Shrewsbury by a sister following the death of his mother. Discovering a love of plants and insects during his time at Cambridge, he subsequently secured a place as a naturalist on the survey ship *HMS Beagle*, which left in 1839 on a voyage to South America.

In the course of the voyage, Darwin began collecting specimens that demonstrated signs of evolution, a phenomenon he clearly identified in finches collected in the Galapagos Islands. He also contracted Chagas' disease from an insect bite and the infection caused him continued bouts of ill health in later years.

After the *Beagle*'s five-year voyage came to an end, Darwin returned to the life of a country gentleman in Kent, and there formulated the three core principles of natural selection in a private memorandum as early as 1844. He did not publish his masterwork, *On the Origin of Species*, however, until 1859. The book aroused considerable controversy, not least in religious circles, but Darwin continued to elaborate on its basic principles, in 1871 publishing notes on the theory of sexual selection.

His last book, *The Formation of the Vegetable Mould Through the Actions of Worms*, appeared in 1881. He died a year later.

MICHAEL FARADAY
(1791–1867)
Physicist and chemist who helped develop the science of electricity

Michael Faraday, perhaps the leading practical scientist of the mid-Victorian period, overcame numerous handicaps to become a key figure in the early development of electrical power. The son of a blacksmith, he received no formal schooling and began his career, aged 12, as an errand boy for a bookbinder. This was a fortuitous choice, since exposure to academic works helped inspire his interest in science, specifically the new science of electricity.

Faraday's introduction to the world of science came about when he was given tickets to a series of lectures by Sir Humphry Davy. He bound and presented his copious lecture notes to Davy. The great scientist subsequently recommended him for the post of chemical assistant at the Royal Institution (where a vacancy had been created as a result of a fight, in the main lecture, between the institution's instrument maker and chemical assistant) and the two men worked together for more than a decade.

Among Faraday's inventions and discoveries was electromagnetic rotation – produced by moving a magnet through a coil of wire – which he used to develop the first electromagnetic motor. He also worked on improvements to the process of making steel, and developed the first portable flame burner – later the Bunsen burner. Faraday became a practical chemist, discovered benzene and, under Davy's instruction, became the first man to liquefy a gas – chlorine.

He was deeply religious and belonged to the Sandemanians, an offshoot of the Church of Scotland that believed the Bible should be interpreted literally and held ritual feasts each Sunday between services. His beliefs made him deeply modest and, although he lived in a grace and favour house in Hampton Court, he declined both a knighthood and the presidency of the Royal Society, preferring to spend his spare time visiting the sick. One of his legacies was a Christmas lecture for children, organised by the Royal Society, which is still given today.

SIR FRANCIS GALTON
(1822–1911)
Polymath, eugenicist, compiler of the first beauty map of Britain

One of the great polymaths of the Victorian age, Sir Francis Galton was an anthropologist, statistician, geneticist, explorer and meteorologist. Praised as a leading scientist of his day, these days he is better remembered for his racial theories.

Born into a family of Quaker gunmakers, Galton was a child prodigy who was reading by the age of two and had devoured Shakespeare by the time he was six. He read mathematics at Cambridge and travelled extensively in eastern Europe and Africa before being inspired by his cousin Charles Darwin's book, *On the Origin of Species*. He devoted the rest of his life to exploring its implications for the human race.

Galton's real achievements were considerable. He discovered the statistical principle of regression to the mean, invented the modern weather map, devised a method for classifying fingerprints, and was the author of the phrase 'nature versus nurture'. He also found time to devise and design an hour-glass speedometer for bicycles, wrote a paper on the ideal length of rope for hanging criminals, and even devised a system for flashing signals to the planet Mars.

Towards the end of his life, Galton became devoted to eugenics. In common with most eminent Victorians, he accepted that upper-class white European males represented the pinnacle of evolution, and grew increasingly concerned that the poorer and supposedly less intelligent members of society were reproducing at a greater rate. Galton suggested that as civilisation developed and life expectancy improved, Darwin's notion of the survival of the fittest would eventually cease to operate in the case of humankind.

Despite being a professed admirer of the figures of African women, Galton urged action such as paying 'superior' couples to marry young and procreate. He proposed that the less able be prevented from marrying until middle age, to reduce the number of their children, with criminals and idiots being confined in humane labour camps and forbidden from ever reproducing.

As part of his research, Galton compiled the first (distinctly unscientific) beauty map of Great Britain. The scientist toured the country, noting the incidence of beautiful girls in each place he visited by making pricks with a needle on a piece of paper concealed in his pocket. He drew the conclusions that London was home to the largest proportion of attractive women, while Aberdeen boasted the highest incidence of ugly ones.

ROBERT PEACOCK GLOAG
(*fl.* 1860)
Hard-headed Scot who introduced the cigarette to Britain

Robert Peacock Gloag, born in Perth, Scotland, was a mere paymaster – an officer in the army in charge of troops' pay – loaned out to Britain's ally, Turkey, during the Crimean War. Most men of his rank were stolid, cautious and unimaginative; the job was generally regarded as a sinecure for the dull and devoted. But when Gloag noticed the Turks smoking tobacco rolled up in twists of paper and rammed into a cardboard mouthpiece, he saw an opportunity. These newfangled 'cigarettes', then unheard-of in Britain, were cheaper than cigars and more convenient to smoke than a pipe – not least on the battlefield.

Returning from the Crimea, Gloag decided to set himself up in business, making cigarettes similar to those he had observed the Turks smoking. Starting out in just a single room in Peckham, Gloag gradually expanded until his 'factory' filled the whole house. Needing more space, he then spilled over into another. By 1870, this 'new' cigarette enterprise filled a row of six properties.

Gloag's cigarettes, filled with strong Turkish tobacco and wrapped in yellow tissue paper, were made by hand. The finished cigarettes – thicker and longer than those sold today – were sold with cane mouthpieces under the brand name 'Sweet Threes'. Gloag delivered the finished product to his handful of waiting customers by dog cart and sold them for five a penny.

The practice soon caught on, and the first cigarette store in London opened for business in 1858, selling not only Gloag's products, but also those supplied by rival Greek and Russian makers. Cigarette smoking was widely frowned on for more than a decade, being regarded as a 'low' activity that was unsuitable for ladies and gentlemen. It was not until the 1870s – with the introduction of smoother Virginia tobacco – that the habit became popular in the UK. By then, Gloag, the pioneer, was already rich and established in a factory in Walworth.

HENRY GRAY
(1825/1827–1861)
Anatomist and author

The eponymous founder of *Gray's Anatomy*, the famous medical text, was a London doctor who became convinced of the need for a comprehensive surgical manual. Henry Gray grew up in almost total obscurity. His father delivered private messages for King William IV and was able to save enough money for Gray to enter St George's Hospital as a student in 1845. There he qualified as a surgeon and won the hospital's triennial essay prize for a dissertation on the nerves of the eye.

Gray's experiences at St George's led him to realise that there was a critical shortage of bodies to anatomise – the demand from medical students for corpses was the reason for the existence of grave robbers such as the notorious Burke and Hare – and convinced him that a new anatomical textbook would be well received. The first edition of his *Anatomy, Descriptive and Surgical* appeared in 1858 and was largely based on personal observation. The book's meticulous attention to detail placed it well above several established rivals and it became a great success.

Before a second edition could be published, Gray contracted smallpox from a nephew and died. But by then he was acknowledged as Britain's greatest expert on the anatomy of the spleen.

JAMES JOULE
(1818–1889)
Physicist who discovered the link between heat and mechanical work

The manager of a Manchester brewery, whose scientific work began as a hobby, James Joule's inquiries into the nature of heat led him to discover its relationship to mechanical work and to the framing of the First Law of Thermodynamics, which states that energy contained in a closed system is conserved, being transferred by heat and work.

Joule was a practical businessman who ran his family brewery until its sale in 1854. His status as a tradesman with no university education led the scientific establishment to reject him for many years. An early paper on the relation of heat and work was dismissed by the Royal Society; Joule was eventually forced to publish an article about it in a Manchester newspaper.

Joule's career finally began to flourish in the 1850s when leading scientists of the day, including Michael Faraday and William Thomson (Lord Kelvin), recognised the importance of his work; Joule was finally elected to the Royal Society in 1850. When, towards the end of his life, he found himself in economic difficulty, Queen Victoria awarded him a pension of £200 a year.

Joule's last major work, for the British Association in 1878, was the determination of the mechanical equivalent of electrical resistance by frictional means. When he died a few years later, his tombstone was engraved with the number '772', the figure produced by this final calculation.

ALAN, DAVID AND THOMAS STEVENSON
(1807–1865, 1815–1886 and 1818–1887)
Scions of Scotland's lighthouse-building dynasty

Before the Stevenson family of Edinburgh started their work, Scotland had few lighthouses, and those that did exist were poorly built and illuminated only by coal fires. Not surprisingly, shipwrecks were common all along the treacherous coast, costing, over the years, thousands of lives. Robert Stevenson (1772–1850) was the first member of the family to make a living as an engineer, and many of the lighthouses he built are still in use today. His three surviving sons (several died in infancy) were all groomed to succeed him, establishing a dynasty that would endure for four generations and save many lives worldwide.

Between them, the three younger Stevensons accounted for nearly 50 lighthouses to add to their father's total of 15. David's sons, David and Charles, continued the dynasty into its third generation, constructing a further three dozen lighthouses between them, but Thomas's son Robert Louis was a severe disappointment to the family, eschewing engineering for literature. He wrote *Treasure Island* in 1880 (see chapter VIII).

Even Robert Louis Stevenson, however, felt pride in his family's achievements. He wrote of the lighthouses: 'When the lights come out at sundown along the shores of Scotland, I am proud to think they burn more brightly for the genius of my father!'

CHARLES WHEATSTONE
(1802–1875)
Inventor of the concertina and the electric telegraph

Thanks largely to the efforts of Michael Faraday, the study of electricity became one of the great passions of the Victorian period, and it was Charles Wheatstone, another scientist specialising in this field, who did more than any other man to render practicable the electric telegraph. This device revolutionised communications a generation before the telephone and had a profound impact on the government as well, making it a far more practicable proposition to control the sprawling British empire.

Around 1830, he also invented the concertina. He followed this triumph by turning to the study of electricity and developing his own primitive telegraph. In 1837 he was visited by an anatomist called William Cooke, who had become convinced that a fortune could be made by developing a more practical apparatus. After some hesitation, due to Wheatstone's belief that scientists should publish their results freely for the benefit of all, the former instrument maker agreed upon a partnership: he would supply the scientific brains and Cooke the commercial knowledge.

The partners were soon able to demonstrate their ability to send a message down an electrical wire running between Euston and Camden Town. A few years later, the first commercial telegraph was opened by the Great Western Railway, between its Paddington headquarters and West Drayton. Later on, the line was extended to Slough.

Public interest in the invention remained slight until 1845, when a message flashed along the telegraph enabled the police to catch a murderer fleeing to London by train. Thereafter, telegraph lines spread rapidly across the country, and Wheatstone was also instrumental in developing the submarine telegraph cables that would unite the continents.

Charles Wheatstone continued his work on electricity into the 1840s and is remembered for inventing the eponymous Wheatstone bridge, which measures electrical resistance. He was also active in the fields of optics and cryptography.

In public, Wheatstone was cripplingly shy; in private he was voluble and often prickly, so much so that he seldom got on well with his partner, Cooke. He died in Paris of an inflammation of the lungs.

CHAPTER VI

❧

VICTORIAN HEROINES

ELIZABETH BARRETT-BROWNING
(1806–1861)
Poet

Elizabeth Moulton-Barrett's father used his fortune, derived from their Jamaican plantations, to buy Hope End, an estate in the Malvern Hills. Although frail, the young Elizabeth seemed healthy enough to enjoy the usual round of privileged childhood pursuits – pony-riding, visiting other families in the vicinity and arranging family theatricals with her 11 siblings. But in 1822, when she was prescribed opium for a nervous disorder, she assumed the role of the exceptionally bright victim of an unspecified illness and, after her mother's death, became a famous invalid.

In the 1830s the family's dwindling fortune and move to London, followed by the death of her favourite brother, Edward, by drowning, turned her into a recluse who spent most of her time in her bedroom.

Self-taught and with a voracious appetite for intellectual pursuits, Moulton-Barrett read Greek, Latin, Hebrew and Italian, and from an early age devoured Paine, Voltaire, Rousseau and Wollenstonecroft. She combined an interest in human rights with a religious mania, which she herself described as 'not the deep persuasion of the mild Christian, but the wild visions of an enthusiast'.

Despite her depression, her literary flame flourished. By the age of 14 she had written her first collection of verse, and when she was 20, her father paid for the printing of *An Essay on Mind*. In 1833 she published a translation of *Prometheus Unbound*, followed by the anonymous *The Seraphim and Other Poems* in 1838. Her poems of 1844 inspired Robert Browning to write, telling her how much he admired her verse. With the aid of a friend, John Kenyon, the two poets met, beginning one of the most famous courtships in English literature. Ecstatic, yet doubtful, she could not believe that he loved her as sincerely as he professed and expressed her doubts in *Sonnets from the Portuguese*. Browning's impassioned response was to elope with her to Italy.

Including her love sonnets in the second edition of her poetry increased Elizabeth Barrett-Browning's popularity immensely, as did her verse novel

Aurora Leigh, and she was seriously considered as a possible Poet Laureate. However, her mind was too preoccupied with great social and political issues, such as the Italian struggle for independence, and the abolition of the slave trade and child labour, to lament its loss to Tennyson. She died in the arms of her husband, aged 55.

ISABELLA BEETON
(1836–1865)
First celebrity chef and domestic goddess

Isabella Beeton was opinionated to say the least. She expressed robust opinions on every aspect of middle-class family life, from charity, child-bearing and cooking equipment to daily routine, dress and servants, inducing an equal measure of respect and paranoia among her readers. Born in Cheapside to Benjamin and Elizabeth Mayson, Beeton was an accomplished musician who was educated at Heidelberg. In 1856, she married Samuel Orchard Beeton, a wealthy publisher, but her career as the Nigella Lawson of her day was surprisingly short-lived, as she died of puerperal fever at the age of 28.

Beeton's first child, Samuel, died in September 1859, but her second son, also named after her husband, survived. Soon after, the first instalment of her cookery book, entitled *The Book of Household Management*, was published. *A History of the Origin, Properties, and Uses of all Things Connected with Home Life and Comfort* was another of her best-selling works. This book contained coloured engravings and 100 recipes for soup, 200 for sauces and 128 for fish, as well her famously presumptuous domestic advice.

The sheer bulk of her published work is accounted for by controversial 'borrowings' from previous writers. Beeton's genius, however, was to bring advice on almost every single aspect of household management together in a single volume.

Beeton, the woman who is alleged to have coined the famous phrase 'a place for everything and everything in its place', lived in a world in which grey areas were unknown. In her opinion, there was a right way and a wrong way to go about things, and woe betide the luckless woman who failed to follow the rules of an increasingly rigid middle-class life.

FRANCES MARY BUSS
(1827–1894)
Educational reformer

Frances Mary Buss, founder of the North London Collegiate School for Ladies and its headmistress for 44 years is, in many ways, the ultimate Victorian heroine. She was the leading figure in the struggle for the education of girls in the second half of the 19th century and paved the way for women's suffrage by devising an educational programme for the girls in her care.

Yet her own start in life was far from ideal. Born in London in 1827, to Robert William Buss, an unsuccessful engraver and illustrator and his wife Frances, Buss was the eldest of 10 children, only five of whom survived childhood. Poor by any standard, she was lucky to be educated locally at dame schools, and began her teaching career at the tender age of 14 in Mrs Wyand's School in Hampstead Road.

Always striving to better herself, Buss took evening classes at the newly established Queen's College in 1849–1850, where she successfully gained certificates in French, German and geography and, perhaps more significantly, was exposed to the radical agenda of Frederick Denison Maurice, the Chartist son of a Unitarian minister and joint founder of the Christian Socialism movement.

Inspired, Buss set up the North London Collegiate School for Ladies in the family home in Camden Street, on 4 April 1850, with just 38 pupils. It aimed to provide education for the daughters of the middle class, making use of visiting lecturers from Queen's College and employing women graduates whenever possible. In 1871, Buss took the decision to change her school from a private establishment to an endowed grammar school, making education accessible to the daughters of many families that had not previously been able to afford private schooling.

Buss was instrumental in the formation of the Association of Head Mistresses, and joined forces with Emily Davies to persuade the authorities to accept women at London University. Together they secured admission of girls to Oxford and Cambridge. In 1865, Buss joined with Dorothea Beale, among others, to form a women's discussion group called the Kensington Society. In 1866 the group formed the London Suffrage Committee and began organising a petition to ask parliament to grant women the vote.

She campaigned with Josephine Butler against pimps' trade in prostitutes, promoted employment for women, pressurised the government to allow women to sit civil service exams, then turned her energies to teacher training. Setting up the Teacher's Guild, she also pushed for the establishment of the Cambridge Training College in 1885.

JULIA MARGARET CAMERON
(1815–1879)
Pioneering photographer

The Isle of Wight does not seem a likely place to have witnessed the birth of modern photography, yet Julia Margaret Cameron, a resident of the island, was one of the world's first photographers, becoming famous in her own time for her portraits.

Cameron took many of her photographs at the home in Freshwater that she had persuaded her husband, Charles, to buy in order to be close to the Poet Laureate, Alfred, Lord Tennyson. She moved in some of the highest circles of society and took photographs of all her (mostly grand) visitors. These included: Darwin, Watts, Thackeray, Lewis Carroll, Robert Browning, William Holman Hunt, Palgrave, Henry Taylor, Edward Lear and the actress

Ellen Terry. As Cameron explained in *Annals of My Glass House* (1874):
'I turned my coal-house into my dark room and a glazed fowl house I had
given to my children became my glass house… the society of hens and
chickens was soon changed for that of poets, prophets, painters and lovely
maidens, who all in turn have immortalised this humble little farm erection.'

Born in Calcutta in 1815, Cameron was educated in France. She returned
to India in 1834 when she was 19 and finally arrived in England with her
husband in 1848. Her career as a photographer began in 1863 when her
husband had to go away on business and she was given a camera by her
daughter. She used large plate negatives, which required sitters to remain
absolutely still for heroic periods of time. As this was practically impossible,
her images often came out soft and out of focus with white streaks; she
chose to embrace these irregularities as part of the overall mood.

Longing to see India again before she died, Cameron left England in 1875
for Ceylon, accompanied by her husband. It was a brave gesture, as she was
at the pinnacle of her fame. The second volume of Tennyson's *Idylls of the
King*, featuring her photographs, had just been published to great acclaim
and she had exhibitions in London and Bournemouth. One of Cameron's last
letters was to Lady Tennyson as she looked back on her achievements: 'It is
a sacred blessing which has attended my photography; it gives a pleasure to
millions and a deeper happiness to very many.'

MARY KINGSLEY
(1862–1900)
Anthropologist, explorer and crocodile wrestler

Rudyard Kipling wrote of Mary Kingsley: 'Being human she must have
been afraid of something, but no-one ever found out what it was.'
Certainly, she did not fit into any Victorian stereotype, enjoying robust
pastimes even from childhood when, in one scientific experiment, she blew
up a tub of manure in an attempt to make gunpowder and spattered a line

of clean clothes. Adventure was in Kingsley's blood. Her father was an anthropologist and her Uncle Gerald was a sea captain who perished on the high seas following an 18-month ordeal in a fever-wracked vessel. At 30, Kingsley took up her father's researches where he had left off and travelled to Africa. She specialised in 'fetish and fish' and discovered many new species, especially of the latter.

Journeying deep into the Gabon, then inhabited by the deadly cannibals the Fang, Kingsley was not only the first woman to enter the territory, but was also the first European. Protected by an escort of Fang warriors on her journey, she alighted at one village where the chief's hut was filled with bags of drying human ears, toes, hands and numerous other scraps of flesh which she euphemistically termed 'other parts'. At the end of her time in Africa, Kingsley overlooked the cultural differences between them and pronounced the Fang 'an uncommonly fine sort of being'.

Not content with these feats, she climbed the 13,760-foot peak of Mount Cameroon by the difficult south-east face and, in a further quest for adventure, departed for the Boer War to nurse soldiers, eventually dying of fever in the field. However, the most enduring image of Kingsley comes from the occasion in Africa when a crocodile managed to hook its front feet into her canoe. She whacked the offending beast fiercely with her paddle, finally dislodging its grip and forcing it to slink back into the water.

ALICE PLEASANCE LIDDELL
(1852–1934)
Muse to the Reverend Charles Dodgson and 'Alice' of the books

Alice Pleasance Liddell arrived in Christ Church College, Oxford, in 1865, when her father was appointed Dean. There the Liddells met a young mathematics lecturer and sub-librarian, the Reverend Charles Lutwidge Dodgson (1832–1898), who was photographing the cathedral. Despite his pronounced stammer, Alice was not put off and became one of

Dodgson's firm 'child friends' and the model for his famous *Alice* books. She also became the cause of seemingly never-ending gossip about his sexuality.

Dodgson was a man who was ordained deacon aged 29 in 1861, yet he never took the final step to priesthood. He enjoyed photographing young children completely nude and, with their parents' permission, took dozens of pictures of Alice and her sisters, Lorina and Edith. Yet the pictures often had a sinister undertone. For example, it is difficult not to look at the photograph of Alice Liddell as 'Beggar Child' without some degree of distaste. She is photographed up against a mossy stone wall in the Deanery at Christ Church and has clearly been instructed to lift her ragged skirt to reveal her knee and a touch of thigh. This, even at a time when character photographs were encouraged, bordered on scandalous.

During her 9th and 10th years, nonetheless, Dodgson and Liddell were firm friends and it was allegedly during a picnic in 1862, heading from Oxford to Godstow, that he first told her *Alice's Adventures Under Ground*. In 1863, Sir John Tenniel agreed to draw the now world-famous illustrations and Dodgson gave Alice the finished book as a Christmas present on 26 November 1864, almost two and a half years after she had asked him to write it down. By this time he had written a longer version, *Alice's Adventures in Wonderland*, published in 1865 under the pen name of Lewis Carroll. Yet when its sequel, *Through the Looking Glass*, was published in 1872, all ties between Dodgson and Alice had been severed.

Lord Salisbury gives us a strong indication as to the source of the rift in June 1863: 'They say that Dodgson has half gone out of his mind in consequence of being refused by the real Alice. It looks like it.' If this were the case, then Dodgson would have proposed marriage to the 11-year-old girl at the age of 31. Dodgson's diaries are missing for 18 April 1858 to 8 May 1862, presumably destroyed by his heirs, which means there is no physical evidence to support the suggestion of a spurned proposal. But a summary of one of the missing pages for 27–29 June 1863 (which seems to cover the period of the break) and written either by Dodgson's niece Violet Dodgson, or Philip Dodgson Jacques, reads: 'LC learns from Mrs Liddell that he is supposed to be using the children as a means of paying court to the governess – he is also supposed [unreadable] to be courting Ina.' If true, this would throw an entirely new light on the tale, but as the note comes from a source within a family involved in destroying a number of documents to preserve Dodgson's heritage, a whiff of cover-up lingers around the whole affair.

Alice married Reginald Hargreaves in 1880, at the age of 28, and they had three sons: Alan Knyveton Hargreaves, Leopold Reginald 'Rex' Hargreaves (both killed in action in World War I) and Caryl Liddell Hargreaves, who survived to have a daughter of his own.

ELISA LYNCH
(c. 1835–1886)
Power behind the Paraguayan throne

Elisa Lynch, an ambitious Irish courtesan, persuaded her paramour, General Don Francisco Solano López Carillo, the 'perpetual dictator' of Paraguay, that he was the Napoleon of South America. Emboldened by her flattery, López declared war simultaneously on Brazil, Argentina and Uruguay, all countries more powerful than his own. The resultant War of the Triple Alliance (1864–1870) caused by his megalomania, saw the Paraguayan population reduced from about 525,000 to 221,000, of whom only 29,000 were adult males.

López died in battle, leading a handful of his surviving troops, and Lynch fled to Paris, where she died of cancer of the stomach. Years later, her body was exhumed and returned to her adoptive country, where it has become a nationalist shrine in the capital, Asunción, celebrating Paraguay's pluck in the face of overwhelming odds.

But what of the origins and rise of 'La Lynch', who led her adoptive nation to doom and glory? Her exact date of birth is uncertain. She claimed to have been born 'of honourable and wealthy parents' with bishops, magistrates and a vice-admiral of the fleet as part of her extended family. What is known is that in 1850 she left Ireland for Paris, where she met and married a medic, Lieutenant Xavier de Quatrefages, on furlough from Algeria. She was packed off to the cantonment bungalows of a grim army town in Algeria. Three years later she left, pleading ill health, but with many rumours surrounding her departure, the strongest being that she had eloped with a Russian to Paris.

On her return to France gossip had spread and Lynch was said to have turned courtesan, ruining one 'Lord L', toying with a Spanish aristocrat and driving a banker to suicide with her red-gold ringlets and 'tall, delicate and flexible' figure. She was said to have bedded 'hundreds', spent 'fortunes', 'run gaming tables' and 'sold her sexual services as language mistress' to members of the foreign embassies on the Champs-Elysées.

As the Russians began to quit Paris in the winter of 1853 in the run-up to the Crimean War, Lynch was left behind. Once again, we know that Lynch was definitely 'top end', appearing in a salon run by Madame La Veuve Dumont on the Rue Tonchet, where the price of a 'special allegiance' was 10,000 French francs or more per month.

Enter General Don Francisco Solano López Carillo, eldest son of the president of Paraguay. He had come to Europe to seek support for his country against the newly united Argentina and the empire of Brazil. From their first meeting, López was hooked: 'Her companion led her back to her sea... [López] was sitting between Madame Téophile and his cherie, a true Venus. Between them, he looked like a fly floating in a glass of milk.'

EMMELINE PANKHURST
(1857–1928)
Suffragette

L ooking at the best-known portrait of Emmeline Pankhurst, standing in her drawing room, with her dreamy gaze and romantically draped velvet gown, it is difficult to picture her doing anything radical – yet everyone identifies her with the British Suffragette Movement, which called for women to receive the vote in the period that immediately preceded World War I.

Pankhurst's vocal style, both charismatic and blunt, was completely at odds with her outward image. The young Rebecca West described hearing Pankhurst in full flow: 'Trembling like a reed, she lifted up her hoarse, sweet voice on the platform, but the reed was of steel and it was tremendous.'

The child of abolitionist parents, she was born Emmeline Goulden and married a barrister, Dr Pankhurst, an advocate of women's suffrage. Pankhurst founded the Women's Franchise League in 1889, but following her husband's death in 1898, launched the much more militant Women's Social and Political Union, with its famous white, purple and green colours. The union advocated violent protest, such as arson, picture slashing and window smashing, and its members included Emily Davison, who was trampled to death by the king's horse in the 1913 Epsom Derby. Two of Pankhurst's daughters, Christabel and Sylvia, also joined the sisterhood while a third, Adela, emigrated to Australia where she was politically active first in the Communist Party of Australia and then, bizarrely, the Australia First Movement, with its undoubted extreme right-wing tendencies.

Imprisoned many times for the cause, Pankhurst endured force-feeding after going on a hunger strike, but she did not experience the same privations as her working-class activists. Perhaps inevitably, her advocacy of civil disobedience caused splits within the movement. However, the idea of suffrage as a revolutionary pageant, complete with night time torch-lit processions, flower-bedecked carts to collect women from jail and immense 'gatherings' to promulgate the word, was very much Pankhurst's legacy.

Her autobiography, *My Own Story*, was published in 1914, putting forward her version of events. In the early months of World War I she helped to mastermind the infamous 'white feather' campaign, in which women presented men in civilian clothes with a feather to indicate they thought them cowards. Many industries were worried about the economic implications of losing so many young men to the army and here Pankhurst saw an opportunity. With the approval of David Lloyd George, she organised a parade of 30,000 women, costing £2,000, to encourage employers to let women take over men's jobs in industry.

After a number of ill-thought-out compromises, women finally achieved universal suffrage in the UK in 1928, the year that Pankhurst died.

MARY SEACOLE
(1805–1881)
Angel of the Crimean War

Officially one of the greatest black Britons ever, Mary Seacole was a heroine of the Crimean War, where she nursed the wounded. Born Mary Jane Grant, in Kingston, Jamaica, in 1805, her father was a Scottish soldier and her mother a Jamaican mulatto who kept a boarding house for invalid soldiers, and who taught Seacole her exceptional nursing skills.

Being of mixed race, although technically 'free' in Jamaica, Seacole had few civil rights and could not vote or hold public office. When her husband died in 1844, after only eight years of marriage, she realised that there was little to keep her in the land of her birth. Fear of the unknown was not a factor. She had visited many other Caribbean islands before her marriage, including Cuba, Haiti and the Bahamas, as well as Central America and Britain. On these trips she added to her knowledge of island medicine by assimilating European medical ideas, and would later publish the story of her extensive travels in *The Wonderful Adventures of Mrs Seacole in Many Lands*.

When Seacole travelled to England in 1854, she approached the recruiting agents for Florence Nightingale's hospital at Scutari and the Crimea Fund, asking to be sent out to the conflict, but she was refused due to her ethnicity. Frustrated, her reaction was both acute and poignant: 'Did these ladies shrink from accepting my aid because my blood flowed beneath a somewhat duskier skin than theirs? Tears flowed down my foolish cheeks as I stood in the fast-thinning streets.'

Undaunted, the 48-year-old Seacole set off on a self-funded trip to the front, becoming known as 'Mother Seacole' and establishing the British Hotel near Balaclava to provide 'a mess-table and comfortable quarters for sick and convalescent officers'. There, Mother Seacole served sponge cake and lemonade, writing sadly: 'They all liked the cake, poor fellows, better than anything else: perhaps because it tasted of "home".'

At the conclusion of hostilities, Seacole returned to England destitute and with her health damaged by the privations imposed during the war. Fortunately, the press highlighted her plight and a grand military fundraising festival was held over four nights at the Royal Surrey Gardens, supported by lords, military commanders and almost 1,000 artistes. Little is known of her later life, but in the 1870s she became both a friend and a masseuse to the Princess of Wales.

BEATRICE WEBB
(1858–1943)
Fabian socialist

Beatrice Webb and her husband, Sidney, were two of the greatest architects of the Labour movement. Yet the young Beatrice, with very little formal schooling, was an unlikely candidate for this accolade, even though her grandfather was Richard Potter, the radical MP for Wigan. Born at Standish House in Gloucestershire, her father was a successful railway entrepreneur, seemingly the embodiment of the capitalist dream.

In 1883 Beatrice Potter, as she was known then, joined the Charity Organisation Society (COS), which attempted to provide Christian help to those living in poverty. She saw that the causes of poverty – low standards of education, housing and public health – needed to be tackled and she accepted a job as a researcher for a rubber entrepreneur turned social reformer named Charles Booth. She investigated dockworkers, Jewish immigration and sweated labour in the tailoring trade, published her observations in the journal, *The Nineteenth Century*, and as a result was invited to testify before the House of Lords. While researching a book on the Lancashire cooperative societies, Potter met and married the like-minded Sidney Webb in 1892. Using her £1,000 annuity, Sidney gave up work and they both became deeply involved in the Fabian Society, which counted Annie Besant, Walter Crane and George Bernard Shaw as members. Their views were enshrined in two books that they co-wrote, *The History of Trade Unionism* (1894) and *Industrial Democracy* (1897). Fate, in the form of Henry Hutchinson, a wealthy solicitor from Derby, provided the Fabian Society with the means to develop. When he left the society £10,000, the Webbs suggested the money be used to start a new university with a socialist agenda. The London School of Economics and Political Science (LSE) was established in 1895.

Moving into the national arena, and always putting social good before personal politics, the couple redefined local government in an 11-volume work on the subject (published over 23 years), merged the Fabian Society into the Labour movement to win seats in the House of Commons for the likes of Kier Hardie in the 1900 General Election, and worked with the winning Conservative Party to draft the 1902 Education Act. If that wasn't enough, they started a new political weekly, *The New Statesman*, in 1913, and Sidney entered parliament for Labour in 1923. He became president of the Board of Trade under Ramsay McDonald a year later. In 1929 he was granted the title Baron Passfield. On a point of principle, however, Beatrice refused to accept the title of 'Lady'.

CHAPTER VII

THE LITERARY ELITE

THE BRONTË SISTERS
CHARLOTTE, EMILY and ANNE
(1816–1855, 1818–1848 and 1820–1849)
Sisters of literary greatness

The Brontë family is probably the greatest literary family Britain has ever produced, and Haworth Parsonage, in Yorkshire – isolated as it was on the bleak moors – enclosed them in an intense inner world in which they created two works of undoubted genius: *Jane Eyre*, written by Charlotte in 1847, and *Wuthering Heights*, written by Emily in 1847. Anne, regarded by many as underrated, wrote *The Tenant of Wildfell Hall* in 1848.

Whether blessed by the touch of genius or not, all the family seemed to write, and both their opium-riddled brother Branwell and their intellectual, driven father, the Reverend Patrick Brontë, saw their works in print. Although famous primarily for their novels, the Brontës first made their appearance in a poetry book called *Poems by Currer, Ellis and Acton Bell* (1846). The book contained 21 poems each by Emily and Anne and 19 by Charlotte. Only two copies were ever sold.

In this volume, Emily's is the breakaway voice of unbridled passion and longing that so shocked early biographers and critics when the work was revealed as that of the daughters of a clergyman. Emily's 'Cold in the earth – and the deep snow piled above thee' seems almost too mature to have been the work of the then teenager's imagination. But the year's progress at Haworth was stultifyingly slow, so the family were forced to create fantasy worlds as children, splitting themselves into citizens of 'Angria' (Charlotte and Branwell) and 'Gondal' (Anne and Emily) and writing a number of tiny books designed to be read by Branwell's toy soldiers, but not by adults.

Their one early venture into the outside world proved disastrous. In 1824, the sisters attended the Clergy Daughters' School at Cowan Bridge, near Kirkby, Lonsdale. The experience, which provided Charlotte with a model for the infamous Lowood School in *Jane Eyre*, ended when her eldest sister, Maria, was sent home poorly and died at the parsonage in May 1825, aged 11. Ten-year-old Elizabeth returned home soon afterwards, only to die on 15 June.

The three remaining girls were expected to earn their living as governesses. To escape this grim destiny, the sisters tried (and failed) to jointly set up a school, but the project did result in Emily and Charlotte travelling to the Pensionnat Heger in Brussels to learn languages, which inspired Charlotte's mature work *Villette*.

However, they were soon back at Haworth, Charlotte suffering from the pains of unrequited love and Emily simply glad to be home. The whole family died very young, with Branwell succumbing to tuberculosis at the age of 31, swiftly followed by Emily and Anne, then Charlotte last, in the third month of pregnancy, aged 39.

ROBERT BROWNING
(1812–1889)
Romantic poet and playwright

B rought up in a comfortable Surrey home filled with 6,000 arcane books collected by his father, a well-paid clerk at the Bank of England, Robert Browning had a conservative upbringing. His grandmother's Creole blood was the only anomaly in an otherwise typical middle-class English childhood. In 1833, his family paid for his first major work, *Pauline: A Fragment of a Confession*, to be printed. Browning was embarrassed by this, prefacing the 1888 edition with the remark: 'Twenty years' endurance of an eyesore seems long enough.'

Visiting Italy for the first time in 1834, the poet was smitten. Like Matthew Arnold, Browning spent his life writing weighty romantic poetry, receiving acclaim for 'Paracelsus'. His early work was not well received by critics, with 'Sordello', a lengthy piece of blank verse about an obscure feud in medieval Italy, being so badly received that he was ever afterwards derided.

The effect on Browning's career was catastrophic. He was shunned by many of the literati, taking over 30 years to be rehabilitated by *The Ring and the Book* (1868), a 12-volume narrative poem, based on a murder case from 1690s

Rome. Despite professional disappointments, Browning's personal life gave him great pleasure. His romance with Elizabeth Moulton-Barrett resulted in an elopement to Italy and the birth of a son, Robert Weidemann Browning. The poet returned to Italy after his wife's death in 1878. He died at his son's home, Ca'Rezzonico in 1889 on the day his last volume, *Asolando*, was published. He was buried in Westminster Abbey, next to Alfred, Lord Tennyson.

WILLIAM WILKIE COLLINS
(1824–1889)
Author of The Woman in White

William Wilkie Collins was as much of a character as many of the heroes and heroines in his famous 'sensation' novels, *The Moonstone* and *The Woman in White*. He became so addicted to laudanum, a mixture of alcohol and opium, that he experienced the paranoid delusion of being constantly accompanied by a doppelgänger, 'Little Wilkie', and a monstrous green woman who sprouted a pair of tusks. In *The Moonstone,* Collins writes vividly of the effects of opium and opium addiction and his consumption of products such as Dalbey's Carminitive and Mother Bailey's Quieting Syrup (opium-based solutions) during this time increased to the extent that Collins had no memory of writing whole sections of the work.

Later in life, Collins suffered a number of other physical ailments. These ranged from rheumatic gout – which he believed had attacked his brain – to less alluring ailments, as his bank manager, Charles Ward, found out when Collins confided in him: 'I have been suffering torments with a boil between my legs and write these lines with the agreeable prospect of a doctor coming to lance it. I seem destined, God help us, never to be well.'

Born in London, the son of a well-known landscape artist, Collins left school and drifted around, trying, at first, an apprenticeship at a tea merchants and then entering Lincoln's Inn to study law, while flirting with alternative careers as a novelist and painter.

His first book, *Memoirs of the Life of William Collins, RA*, a tribute to his father, was published in 1848, and he exhibited a picture at the Royal Academy in 1849. But it was with the publication of his first novel, *Antonina*, in 1850 that his writing career began in earnest. Collins wrote on what he called 'the secret theatre of home', the plight of women, and on domestic and social issues, yet his own personal life was irregular, living on and off with a widow, Mrs Caroline Graves. Collins also fathered three children by Martha Rudd, whom he met after splitting with Mrs Graves in 1868. After two years apart, Mrs Graves returned to Collins, who juggled both relationships until he died in 1889. He was laid to rest in Kensal Green Cemetery.

JOSEPH CONRAD
(1857–1924)
Seaman, gunrunner and novelist

Born Jósef Konrad Korzeniowski, to Polish parents in what is now the Ukraine, exiled with his family to Siberia as a child and orphaned at the age of 12, Joseph Conrad had none of the qualifications one would expect of a successful English novelist. A sailor at the age of 17 in the French Merchant Navy who spoke English as a third language, it's amazing that Conrad was able to triumph over his disadvantages.

The family was a literary one – his father was a politically active translator of French and English works – but the young Jósef dreamed of adventure at sea. During an extraordinarily active youth he sailed to the Caribbean, Australia, the South Pacific and even up the Congo, experiences that gave him the material he later moulded into powerful works of fiction.

By 1886, when he was finally made captain of his own ship, Conrad was serving with the British Merchant Navy and had anglicised his unwieldy Polish name. He had worked briefly as a gunrunner in the Caribbean and may well have had some involvement in terrorism and espionage, both subjects he covered extensively in his writings. Conrad came ashore for the final time at the age of 36 and immediately embarked on a literary career. His earliest works included *Nostromo* (1904), about a revolution in South America, and *The Secret Agent* (1907), but he is probably best known for *Heart of Darkness* (1902), a novella set in what appears to be the Congo and which concerns itself with the horrors visited on Africa by brutal colonialists. Conrad died of a heart attack in 1924.

CHARLES DICKENS
(1812–1870)
Prolific novelist and social critic

E ven the unhappiest of times can prove to be a great source of inspiration and the later childhood of Charles Dickens, marred by poverty, undoubtedly resulted in the creation of much of the famous novelist's most celebrated works.

Dickens was not born into poverty. His father, a naval clerk, was actually a member of the lower middle class, and the writer's early youth was principally a happy time; he attended a good school, was largely unsupervised at home, and read voraciously. At the age of 12, however, the Dickens family's habit of living just beyond its means landed both parents in a debtors' prison and Charles went to work in a factory, pasting labels onto pots of bootblack for a salary of six shillings a week. He remained in the factory for nearly three years, forced to retain his position even after his parents were released.

At 15, Dickens began work as a law clerk and was taught the art of stenography. He became a court reporter, then a journalist, and took to contributing to several journals. He made his name with the publication of the comic serial *The Pickwick Papers* when he was 24. He continued to write fiction, almost always in serial form, for the rest of his life, producing 15 novels and numerous short stories and travelogues. Dickens's works, more often than not, display an obsession with the conditions of the working poor inspired, in part, by his own experiences. The writer's own position soon altered for the better with his literary success and he became very wealthy.

Dickens was married to Catherine Hogarth in 1836, and the couple had 10 children. But by the late 1850s, the marriage was over and the writer spent much of his time with actress Ellen Ternan, 28 years his junior and almost certainly his mistress. In 1865, while travelling with Ternan, Dickens survived a rail crash near Folkestone in which 10 passengers were killed. The shock sharply reduced his productivity and he died five years later to the day.

GEORGE ELIOT
(1819–1880)
Leading English novelist and pen name of Mary Anne Evans

Mary Anne Evans (who wrote, like many female contemporaries, under a male pseudonym) was a bewitchingly interesting and clever woman of pronounced liberal views.

As George Eliot, Evans wrote *Middlemarch* (1872), *The Mill on the Floss* (1860), *Silas Marner* (1861), *Felix Holt* (1866) and *The Radical* (1866), books that concern themselves with the problems of outcasts and outsiders. Her interest in such characters may have been inspired by her own lonely childhood, due to an enforced separation from her brother and playmate, Isaac, who had been despatched to boarding school.

Eliot's home life was at least as scandalous as her literary philosophy. In her mid-30s she took up with a decidedly married literary critic, George Henry Lewes, with whom she lived happily for 25 years. The relationship was eventually accepted by the couple's friends and the identity of 'George Eliot' became an open secret in literary circles.

In 1879, Lewes died after an agonising illness and a year later Eliot, then 60, accepted a proposal of marriage from the 40-year-old John Cross, her business manager. The marriage only lasted seven months before Eliot herself died of kidney failure at the age of 61.

THOMAS HARDY
(1840–1928)
Creator of the 'Wessex' novels

Thomas Hardy was born in Higher Brockhampton near Dorchester. His father was a stonemason and his mother was well read and ambitious for her son, who showed signs of brilliance from an early age. All his great novels were set in the semi-fictional county of Wessex, including *Far From the Madding Crowd* (1874) and *The Return of the Native* (1878), in which the humble protagonists battled fruitlessly against fate and a merciless universe.

Hardy's bleak view of life also applied to his own family's prospects. In 1870 he wrote: 'Mother's notion and also mine; that a figure stands in our van with arms uplifted, to knock us back from any permanent prospect we indulge in as profitable.'

Passionate in his political opinions and knowledgeable about rural ways of life, Hardy opposed the Corn Laws vehemently, as he saw them as an attack on the meek. But religion left him untouched, even though in his youth he dressed up as a child-vicar to preach sermons to his cousin and grandmother. He later wrote: 'I have been looking for God for 50 years, I think if he had existed I should have discovered him.'

Hardy trained as an architect, and it was while restoring the church of St Juliot in North Cornwall that he met his first wife, Emma Gifford, the heroine of *A Pair of Blue Eyes* (1873), whom he married in 1874. With a parvenu's pride, he proclaimed her the daughter of an archdeacon in *Who's Who* and took particular pleasure from his eventual entry into the Athenaeum Club in London. Here, the 'high' families and church members that he had written about so bitterly abounded. Acutely sensitive to social slight, Hardy gave up writing novels after a bishop burned *Jude the Obscure* (1895), due to the 'immoral' (or non-marital) nature of the relationship between Jude and his cousin, Sue. As a result, the book was popularly referred to as 'Jude the Obscene'. It was not the first time that the author had reacted extremely, having torn up his first novel, *The Poor Man and the Lady*, in 1867 when he could not find a publisher.

Hardy could be ghoulish and insensitive when speaking of others. In 1856, he saw the hanging of Martha Brown of Birdsmoorgate, a tranter's wife who had killed her husband out of jealousy. In 1925, when asked by his friend Lady Hester Pinney for details, he wrote: 'I remember what a fine figure she showed against the sky as she hung in the misty rain, and how the tight black silk gown set off her shape as she wheeled half-round and back.' Then, in the next sentence: 'I hope that you have not felt the cold much...'

When Emma died in 1912 he was traumatised, even though they had been estranged, partly due to the furore over *Jude*. After a period of mourning Hardy met and married Florence Dugdale, some 40 years his junior, in 1914, and stayed with her until his death from pleurisy in 1928.

Controversial even in death, a row broke out over Hardy's funeral when his family and friends wanted him to be buried at Stinsford, Dorset, but his executor, Sir Sydney Carlyle Cockerell, insisted on Poets' Corner. A compromise was reached: his heart was buried in Stinsford and his ashes were interred in Westminster Abbey.

GERARD MANLEY HOPKINS
(1844–1889)
Poet and religious convert

With the boyish gusto often found in Gerard Manley Hopkins' letters to relations and friends, he once wrote to fellow poet Robert Bridges: 'What fun if you were a classic!' Ironically, it was he, and not Bridges, who entered the poetic pantheon and proved to be the genuine original of the two.

Born in Essex, the son of a devout middle-class couple, Hopkins won the Poetry Prize at Highgate School in 1860, where he cultivated a reputation for eccentricity and self-denial. For example, when he was beaten with the headmaster's riding whip, he rebelled with an almost hysterical vigour. On another occasion, disgusted by how much people drank, he won a wager by abstaining from drinking any fluid for a whole week.

When Hopkins went up to Balliol College, Oxford, he was initially an ardent Puseyite – Edward Pusey was a leading Anglican who pushed for the assimilation of Catholic dogma into Protestantism. He defended the Anglican 'middle way' against the flight to Catholicism by John Henry Newman. But even he eventually succumbed to conversion, in October 1866, entering the Novitiate of the Society of Jesus in 1868 with the aim of becoming a Jesuit priest. Hopkins immediately burned most of his poetry as incompatible with his new life, vowing to write no more verse 'as not belonging to my profession, unless by the wish of my superiors'.

Fortunately, in 1872, he came across the writings of Duns Scotus, who, unlike St Thomas Aquinas, attached great importance to individuality and personality. 'From this time,' he wrote, 'I was flush with a new enthusiasm', and he began to write the slender body of work that remains today.

Between 1877 and 1881, Hopkins, aware of his flagging health, served as a select preacher, missionary or parish priest in London, Oxford, Liverpool, Glasgow and Chesterfield, following this with a two-year spell teaching Greek and Latin at Stonyhurst College, Blackburn. Hopkins' final appointment was as chair of classics at University College, Dublin, where he was unhappy, finding it an increasing effort to summon the will to write.

Hopkins died in 1889 of typhoid fever complicated by peritonitis. 'The life I lead,' he wrote towards the end of his time, 'is liable to many mortifications, but the want of fame as a poet is not one of them.'

GEORGE SMITH
(1824–1901)

Publisher and visionary behind the Dictionary of National Biography

Inspired by the publication of national biographical collections elsewhere in Europe, publisher George Smith began to work on Britain's first *Dictionary of National Biography* in 1882. His early vision was to create a universal dictionary of notable figures from throughout the world, but his editor Leslie Stephen soon convinced him to concentrate on British subjects for the sake of expediency. The first volume appeared on 1 January 1885 and has been reissued every year since; today it is published by Oxford University Press.

ALFRED, LORD TENNYSON
(ALSO 1ST BARON TENNYSON)
(1809–1892)
Great Victorian poet

Alfred, Lord Tennyson's poetry was steeped in the crises of the age – its conflicts between progress and expansion and nostalgia and religion. Yet despite the beauty and romance of his verse, he had a deeply unlikeable and noticeably racist side, even for its time. In 1865, supporting Governor Edward John Eyre (see chapter III) in the savage suppression of the Jamaican slave rebellion, Tennyson penned the following curt note to the then Prime Minister William Gladstone: 'We are too tender to our savages. We are more tender to blacks than ourselves… niggers are tigers, niggers are tigers.'

The son of a drunkard rector, much of Tennyson's verse was based on classical or mythological themes, although his best regarded poem, 'In Memoriam', was a eulogy for his friend Arthur Hallam, a fellow poet and classmate at Trinity College, Cambridge, whom he had met at a secret society called The Apostles. In 1830, he published his first solo collection of poems, *Poems Chiefly Lyrical*, which included 'Claribel' and 'Mariana', followed in 1833 by *The Lady of Shalott*, a story of a princess who cannot look at the world except through a reflection in a mirror. The volume met with heavy criticism which so discouraged Tennyson that he did not publish again for 10 years. He did continue to write, but was hampered by money worries caused by an unwise investment in an ecclesiastical wood-carving enterprise.

His most famous work is *The Idylls of the King* (1885), a series of narrative poems based on the Arthurian legend. In 1850, Tennyson reached the pinnacle of his career, being appointed Poet Laureate and producing his masterpiece, 'In Memoriam AHH'. That year he also married Emily Sellwood, and they had two sons, Hallam – named after his friend – and Lionel.

In 1855, Tennyson produced one of his best-known works, 'The Charge of the Light Brigade', a dramatic tribute to the British cavalrymen in the Crimean War. Queen Victoria was an admirer of Tennyson's work, and in 1884 made him Baron Tennyson of Blackdown in the County of Sussex and Freshwater on the Isle of Wight, making him the first English writer to be raised to the peerage. He died in October 1892 and was buried at Westminster Abbey.

WILLIAM MAKEPEACE THACKERAY
(1811–1863)
Novelist, journalist and satirist

Plagued by syphilis and a life of constant frustrations that included money worries, concern about his wife's mental stability and a fear of his beloved daughters slipping down the social ladder, William Makepeace Thackeray vented all his angst in his various novels, articles and satires, gaining a reputation for a biting wit. He is chiefly remembered for his social portraits, particularly *Vanity Fair* (1847/48).

Writing in the tradition of Henry Fielding and Tobias Smollett, Thackeray's first book, *The Memoirs of Barry Lyndon, Esq* (1844), was not a popular success and he deeply resented the popularity Dickens enjoyed. In fact, what started as a jostle for ratings between the two later became personal, when Thackeray inadvertently confirmed Dickens' affair with Ellen Ternan. In turn, Dickens took Edmund Yates's side after Yates wrote several impolite things about Thackeray.

Thackeray's father, Richmond, was secretary to the Board of Revenue and his mother, Anne Beecher, had been shipped out to India to marry him, having been told untruthfully by her grandmother that the man she loved, Henry Carmichael-Smyth, had died. The truth was revealed when Richmond

Thackeray inadvertently invited the 'dead' man to dinner. This shock reunion seems to have wrecked the marriage beyond repair. Richmond Thackeray died shortly afterwards in 1815. Henry Carmichael-Smyth finally laid claim to Anne in 1818 and they returned to England.

Thackeray had been sent back to England at the age of five and educated at Charterhouse, or 'Slaughterhouse', as he called it. He then went up to Cambridge but quickly dropped out, travelling for some time on the continent and visiting Paris and Weimar, where he met Goethe. On returning to England he practically became a professional dropout, squandering his inheritance on gambling and two new newspapers, *The National Standard* and *The Constitutional*, which rapidly closed down. Then he studied art in Paris, but found he had no talent for it, sinking into a slough of despondency at the state to which he had been reduced.

A ray of light was his marriage to Isabella Gethin Shaw in 1836, but this was extinguished when she became mentally ill in 1840, suffering from depression and attempting suicide at least once. She bore him daughters, but heartbreakingly lapsed into a semi-vegetative state, while he was doing his best to earn money as editor of *The Cornhill Magazine*. Isabella remained ill for the rest of her life, but she outlived her husband by 30 years.

Thackeray's funeral in Kensal Green Cemetery attracted some 7,000 people. He would have been bitterly amused by the fact he was not buried in Westminster Abbey but that, almost as an afterthought, a memorial bust sculpted by Marochetti was placed there to commemorate him.

ANTHONY TROLLOPE
(1815–1882)
Prolific English novelist and post office innovator

Born to an ill-tempered barrister and a literary mother, Anthony Trollope was an unhappy child who found it difficult to reconcile the poverty of his home life with the pretensions of his elite schooling. Although intelligent and well-educated, attempts at university scholarships failed, and he followed his family to Belgium in 1834, where his parents had moved to escape his father's rising debts. After a brief stint as an assistant teacher in Bruges, he took up a position as a civil servant in the British Post Office and was transferred to Ireland in 1841 where he met and married his English wife, Rose Heseltine.

It was during this period that Trollope first began to write, using the time spent travelling around Ireland on long business trips to produce his early novels; his first was *The Macdermots of Ballycloran* (1847), about a doomed Irish family. It was his fourth novel, *The Warden* (1855), that established Trollope's reputation as a writer. He was transferred back to London by the post office in the mid-1860s, bringing with him the idea for England's first red pillar boxes, which were based on Ireland's green counterparts. By this time, Trollope had started to derive a substantial income from his novels and, when he left the post office in 1867 to unsuccessfully run for parliament, he began to concentrate entirely on his literary output, which was prolific to say the least.

Although much reviled in later years for his systematic approach to literature, he stuck to a rigorous writing schedule, rising at 5am and producing a given number of words before leaving the house. By the time of his death in 1882, he had produced 47 novels, several travel books, biographies, and innumerable short stories and sketches. His last novel, *Mr Scarborough's Family*, was published posthumously in 1883. He is buried in Kensal Green Cemetery near to his contemporary William Wilkie Collins.

OSCAR FINGAL O'FLAHERTIE WILLS WILDE
(1854–1900)
Anglo-Irish playwright, novelist, poet and short story writer

One of the most successful playwrights of his day, Oscar Fingal O'Flahertie Wills Wilde suffered a dramatic downfall after being convicted in a famous 'gross indecency' trial for homosexual acts.

Wilde was born into a Protestant Anglo-Irish family, to Sir William Wilde, Ireland's leading ear and eye surgeon, and his wife Jane, also known as 'Speranza', a successful writer and Irish Nationalist. He was showered with honours as a young man, from the Berkeley Gold Medal at Trinity College, Dublin, to the Newdigate Prize in 1878 for the poem, 'Ravenna'.

While at Oxford, Wilde began to wear his hair long and decorate his rooms with peacock feathers, lilies, sunflowers and blue china. After college he became a leading figure in the Aesthetic movement which promoted 'art for art's sake' and not only influenced literature and the decorative arts, but also persuaded women to unlace their corsets and wear loose, comfortable gowns.

Wilde lived with the society painter Frank Miles for years, but in 1884 he met and married a well-off barrister's daughter, Constance Lloyd, whose yearly allowance of £250 permitted the Wildes to live in relative luxury and bring up two sons, Cyril, born in 1885, and Vyvyan, born in 1886. With money in the bank, a steady outpouring of work followed, from fairy tales such as *The Happy Prince* (1888) to dramas such as *Lady Windermere's Fan* (1892). The latter was a huge success, making the author £7,000 after a triumphant first night to which he sported a green carnation. *Salomé* (1892) was refused a licence by the Lord Chamberlain because it contained biblical characters, and this caused Wilde to erupt in fury, threatening to become a French citizen. Fortunately, several successful plays followed, including his masterpiece, *The Importance of Being Earnest* (1895).

Wilde was preoccupied by the cause of same-sex love espoused in the writings of gay rights campaigner Karl-Heinrich Ulrichs. In letters he referred to the legalisation campaign as 'The cause' and boasted, when he disembarked from an American lecture tour: 'I have the kiss of Walt Whitman still on my lips.' However, Wilde's illicit passions were soon to consume him. In 1891 he became intimate with his most famous lover, Lord Alfred Douglas or 'Bosie', son of John Sholto, 9th Marquess of Queensbury. Relations between Sholto and Wilde became increasingly strained, and on 18 February 1895, the marquess left a card for Wilde at the Albermarle accusing the writer of 'posing as a somdomite' [sic].

Egged on by his lover, Wilde charged Queensbury with criminal libel, committing perjury in the dock. Things did not go well, however, and by the third day, Wilde had to withdraw his case. He was subsequently charged and convicted of gross indecency and sentenced to two years hard labour. After a tour of prisons he ended up in Reading Gaol, where, as Prisoner C33, he wrote a 50,000-word letter to Bosie which he was never allowed to send. On his release, he gave it to an intermediary who published an expurgated version four years after Wilde's death, as *De Profundis*.

Wilde left prison penniless and adopted a new name, Sebastian Melmoth, after the central character in his great-uncle Charles Robert Marturin's novel, *Melmoth the Wanderer* (1820). He spent his last days at the Hotel d'Alsace in Paris. Just a month before his death of cerebral meningitis, Wilde, ever the aesthete, is quoted as saying: 'My wallpaper and I are fighting a duel to the death. One or other of us has got to go.'

CHAPTER VIII

MOULDERS OF YOUNG MINDS

FRANCES HODGSON BURNETT
(1849–1924)
Playwright and author

Frances Hodgson Burnett was an English playwright and author, best known in her own lifetime for romantic novels. Today she is mostly remembered for the children's stories *Little Lord Fauntleroy* (1886), *The Secret Garden* (1888) and *A Little Princess* (1909).

Hodgson Burnett first started to write in order to help her family out of financial difficulties after the death of her father. Her first stories, *Hearts and Diamonds* and *Miss Caruther's Engagement*, were published in *Godey's Lady's Book* in 1868, but her first widely read work was a dialect story, *Surly Tim's Trouble*, which appeared in *Scribner's Magazine* in 1872.

In 1886, she published *Little Lord Fauntleroy*, about an American boy who inherits an English earldom. It was one of the first children's books to cross over to adult readers, with its appealing portrait of a hero with long curls and Wildean velvet suits and lace collars. This book created a new fashion, but it also embroiled Hodgson Burnett in a costly legal case when, in 1888, she was forced to fight for the dramatic rights to *Little Lord Fauntleroy*, establishing a precedent that was incorporated into British copyright law in 1911.

In other respects, her personal life was stormy. Her first marriage to Dr Swan M Burnett in 1873 ended in divorce in 1898, and her second marriage, to her business manager, Stephen Townsend, lasted less than two years. To add to these troubles, she lost her first son Lionel to consumption and was plunged into a period of mourning, only finding relief in spiritualism and by writing a novella about life after death, called *The White People* (1917).

In 1893, Hodgson Burnett published the memoir, *The One I Knew Best of All*. In 1905, she became an American citizen; she moved there for good in 1909 and settled in Long Island, New York, where she lived until her death in 1924. She was buried at Roslyn Cemetery, New York, next to her second son, Vivian. A life-sized effigy of Lionel stands at their feet.

SIR ARTHUR IGNATIUS CONAN DOYLE
(1859–1930)
'The Good Giant' who breathed life into Sherlock Holmes

The son of a chronic alcoholic, Arthur Ignatius Conan Doyle was born on 22 May 1859 in Edinburgh, Scotland. His father was eventually confined to a lunatic asylum and the desperate boy was forced to sign the committal papers on his return from school. Bowed by financial worries, he went to the University of Edinburgh to read medicine, coming under the tutelage of the 'Holmesian' Dr Joseph Bell who taught him the value of observation, logic and deduction.

While still an undergraduate, adventure beckoned in the form of a post as ship's surgeon on the *Hope*, a whaling boat headed for the Arctic. After an unhappy follow-up tour to the west coast of Africa, however, Conan Doyle came home and fell in with an unscrupulous Plymouth doctor – an experience he later wrote about in *The Stark Munro Letters* (1895).

In 1885, Conan Doyle married Louisa Hawkins and started writing the first Sherlock Holmes and Dr Watson story, *A Study in Scarlet* (1887). Combining writing and medicine, he eventually set up a practice in Upper Wimpole Street, but he claimed that not one patient crossed his door.

In 1891, Conan Doyle nearly died as a result of influenza and it was at this time he decided to terminate his medical career and kill off his detective hero at the Reichenbach Falls, Switzerland. This caused 20,000 readers of *The Strand Magazine*, where Holmes's stories appeared, to cancel their subscriptions. Around the same time, Louisa contracted tuberculosis. Conan Doyle nursed her devotedly through the lengthy, chronic illness, despite meeting and falling in love with Jean Leckie, a green-eyed, blonde, mezzo-soprano. He married Jean in 1907, a year after Louisa's death.

During this period, Conan Doyle created a Holmes play, which toured America and ended up at the Lyceum in 1901 to great acclaim; however, the author hardly had time to enjoy its success as he had enlisted as a medical officer in the Boer War. In 1902, King Edward VII knighted Conan Doyle and was delighted to see *The Return of Sherlock Holmes* in

The Strand Magazine in 1903 – albeit featuring the hero as a cocaine addict and frequenter of opium dens.

'The Good Giant' died of angina pectoris in 1930, whispering to his second wife on his deathbed: 'You are wonderful.'

GEORGE ALFRED HENTY
(1832–1902)
Prolific author of boys' fiction

Nowadays George Alfred Henty is deeply unfashionable, but in his day, he was a decidedly popular author, particularly among young boys with fervent imaginations. With very few exceptions, his books have an adolescent boy as the protagonist and a stirring historical setting. Whether it's the French Revolution, the Huguenot Wars or Agincourt, all the favourite stories from history get revisited. In Henty's world a stout heart, a stiff upper lip, the companionship of some good chums and a willingness to engage in fisticuffs to teach a ruffian a lesson were all that was needed to get on in life. These parodies of Englishness unashamedly championed upper-crust British values as the pinnacle of achievement.

Henty is among the most prolific authors of children's books, with 80 to his name, averaging around three books a year. In his lifetime, according to his Scottish publishers, there were 25 million copies of his novels in circulation. His experience as a war reporter stood him in good stead for adding colour to the battle scenes, which were surprisingly gory. Slight and quiet as a young child, when he started at Westminster School Henty turned himself into the hero of one of his own stories, taking up boxing and rowing, and suddenly finding favour with his contemporaries as a good fellow who was always ready to help one out of a scrape.

After a year at Cambridge, during which the Crimean War broke out, Henty left for Sebastopol. He worked for the hospital commissariat and wrote long letters home about his experiences – these were published in the *Morning Advertiser* and led to a 10-year stint as roving reporter for *The Standard*, and eventually to his first commission as an author. In old age, Henty continued to present the image of the essence of British manliness and died in a boating accident in Weymouth Harbour in 1902.

THOMAS HUGHES
(1822–1896)
Creator of Tom Brown's Schooldays

A sturdy landowner's son from Uffington in Berkshire, Thomas Hughes' life was turned around by a book that he read while studying to be a lawyer at Oriel College, Oxford – *The Kingdom of Christ* (1838) by Frederick Denison Maurice. In this book, Maurice argued that politics and religion should be inseparable and that the Church, together with driven men, should be involved in addressing social questions.

Hughes became a supporter of Chartism and after the decision by the House of Commons to reject the Chartist Petition in 1848, he formed, together with Maurice and Charles Kingsley, the Christian Socialist movement, with the aim of addressing what they considered to be the reasonable grievances of the working class.

The word was to be spread by two journals, *Politics of the People* (1848–1849) and *The Christian Socialist* (1850–1851), together with a series of pamphlets under the title 'Tracts on Christian Socialism'. Other initiatives included setting up a night school in Little Ormond Yard and helping to form eight Working Men's Associations. These efforts bore fruit when, in 1854, their evening classes were developed into the establishment of the Working Men's College.

Hughes is principally remembered for his 'boy roasting' novel *Tom Brown's Schooldays* (1856), which was based on his own unhappy experiences at Rugby. Sadly, his follow-up novel, *Tom Brown at Oxford*, was less successful. Hughes became a Liberal MP between 1865 and 1874 and principal of the Working Men's College from 1872 to 1883, dying in 1896.

CHARLES KINGSLEY
(1819–1875)
Author of The Water Babies,
Christian Socialist and Chartist

Charles Kingsley is best remembered for his charming book *The Water Babies*, which is both a fairy tale and a passionate social gospel. First published in 1863, it denounced the practice of chimney sweeps sending luckless boys into the houses of the gentry via the chimney flue. Indeed, so powerful was the book's message that the practice was abolished a year later.

Kingsley was born in Holne in Devon, the brother of the novelist Henry Kingsley. He was prodigiously clever, receiving a first in maths from Magdalene, Cambridge, and going straight into the Church where, from 1844, he was the rector of Eversley in Hampshire. From that moment on, Eversley was the centre of his universe, even when he travelled to London to promote Christian Socialism or to discuss his novels *Alton Locke* (1850) and *Yeast* (1851), which popularised the Chartist position. When, in 1860, he was appointed Regius Professor of Modern History at Cambridge, Kingsley used to deliver his lecture, stay overnight and scurry back to his parish as early as possible.

Kingsley was tall and thin, with dark hair and dark eyes. He was addicted to smoking to such an extent that he scattered caches of clay pipes in bushes and under trees around his parish in case he should be forced to step outside a parishioner's home for a quiet puff. Cursed with a stammer, Kingsley had a nervous, excitable, hot-headed temperament undercut by a loving side, which came through in his marriage to Fanny Grenfell.

Here he made a happy choice, although they almost got off to a poor start after he confessed to premarital liaisons with fallen women. Fanny, impressed by Kingsley's guilt over the revelation, readily forgave him everything. During a long engagement, he wrote a life of St Elizabeth of Hungary, illustrating the story with pictures of young, naked women being tortured by monks. He died, aged 56, worn out by smoking and hyperactivity, and was buried at his beloved Eversley.

RUDYARD KIPLING
(1865–1936)
Arguably Britain's greatest short story writer

Rudyard Kipling was an arch-exponent of the British empire, full of racial prejudices which today seem almost incomprehensible to us. Yet, despite this, Kipling was a brilliant literary stylist, becoming the first Englishman to receive the Nobel Prize for Literature (1907).

He was born in Bombay, India, into an artistic family. His mother was a sister-in-law of Edward Burne-Jones and his father was an arts and crafts teacher at Jeejeebhoy School of Art, Bombay. He left India at the age of six and was sent to a very unhappy foster home in Southsea, later describing his terrible experiences in the short story *Baa Baa, Black Sheep* (1888). In 1878, Kipling entered United Services College in north Devon, but his plans to enlist in the military were scuppered by his poor eyesight. He later immortalised the whole episode in his highly popular children's book, *Stalky & Co* (1899).

Kipling returned to India in 1882, where he worked as a journalist in Lahore for *The Civil and Military Gazette* (1882–1887) and as an assistant editor and overseas correspondent in Allahabad for *The Pioneer* (1887–1889). The stories written during his last two years in India were collected in *The Phantom Rickshaw* (1888).

Kipling returned to London in 1889 and was hailed as the new Charles Dickens. He tried to settle into urban life and published a number of stories and poems. In 1892 he married Caroline Starr Balestier and moved with her to Vermont in the United States. The death of his daughter led to another move, this time to Burwash in Sussex, where he eventually settled. During these years, Kipling produced some of his greatest works, including *The Jungle Book* (1894), *Kim* (1901) and *Just So Stories* (1902).

In 1899, Kipling spent several months in South Africa and liked it there so much that he returned a number of times before his death in 1936.

EDWARD LEAR
(1812–1888)
Glorious writer of nonsense verse

E dward Lear was one of 21 children. As a child he had attacks of epilepsy and depression, and throughout his life suffered from asthma, bronchitis and poor eyesight. Weak he may have been, but by 15 he was earning money from teaching drawing and selling sketches. He also worked as a draughtsman for the Zoological Society, illustrated a book about parrots and completed drawings for *Tortoises, Terrapins and Turtles*.

In 1832, fate smiled in the form of the 13th Earl of Derby, who commissioned Lear to create a collection of drawings of rare birds in the Knowsley Hall menagerie on Merseyside. The earl's backing meant he could travel extensively in Italy and Greece, where he made collections of drawings and oil paintings. From these he published several travel books including *Sketches of Rome* (1842) and *Illustrated Excursions in Italy* (1846). Lear invented nonsense limericks and tales to amuse the earl's children. He illustrated these with sketches and later published them in *A Book of Nonsense* (1846) under the pseudonym 'Derry Down Derry'.

After living in Rome for 10 years, Lear returned to England in 1846 to give drawing lessons to Queen Victoria at Osborne House and Buckingham Palace. He left three years later for Malta in the company of Franklin Lushington, a young barrister and the brother of the government secretary in Malta. The pair explored southern Greece together before Lear returned to London to study painting at the Royal Academy Schools. In 1855, Lear settled in Corfu, where Lushington had just been appointed to the Supreme Court of Justice. On arrival he took on an Albanian servant, Giorgio Kokali, who stayed with him for 27 years.

For the next 20 years, he travelled around the Mediterranean and Middle East, composing 'The Owl and the Pussycat' for John Addington Symonds' daughter, Janet, whom he met in Corfu. Eventually, he settled in San Remo in Casa Emily – named after Emily Tennyson – where Lushington was a regular guest. Lear died of bronchitis in 1888.

EDITH NESBIT
(1858–1924)
Famous children's novelist and
founder member of the Fabian Society

Educated in France, Edith Nesbit was the daughter of a successful schoolmaster who died when she was six. She married Hubert Bland, a young writer with radical political opinions, after falling pregnant at 19. The baby was born two months after they were married on 22 April 1880.

Nesbit and Bland were both ardent socialists and in 1884 they founded a debating group, the Fabian Society, with Edward Pease, Havelock Ellis and Frank Podmore. Soon after, well-known left wingers – including Eleanor Marx, Annie Besant, George Bernard Shaw and the Webbs – began attending meetings. There was a limit to how far left the couple wanted to move. A brief flirtation with the Social Democratic Federation in 1885 was abandoned when Nesbit found the views of its leader, HH Hyndman, too revolutionary.

A woman of radical ideas, Nesbit was severely tested in 1885, when she gave birth to a second child named Fabian. Alice Hoatson, the assistant secretary of the Fabian Society, moved in with Nesbit and her husband, who had an affair with Alice and impregnated her, too. Nesbit, showing considerable restraint, brought up the resulting baby as her third child.

Nesbit was a regular lecturer and writer on socialism throughout the 1880s. However, she gave less time to these activities after she became a successful children's writer. Her most famous novels include *The Wouldbegoods* (1901), *Five Children and It* (1902), *The Phoenix and the Carpet* (1904) and *The Railway Children* (1906). She also had a collection of her political poetry published, *Ballads and Lyrics of Socialism* (1908). Yet according to Noel Streatfield, Nesbit wrote to support her family of five and 'did not particularly like children, which might explain why the ones that she created in her books are so entirely human. They are intelligent, vain, aggressive, humorous, witty, cruel, compassionate... in fact, they are like adults, except for one difference... they cannot control their environment.'

Nesbit could also be shockingly blunt. For example, in 1884, she said of George Bernard Shaw: 'He... is the grossest flatterer I ever met, is horribly untrustworthy as he repeats everything he hears, and does not always stick to the truth, and is very plain like a long corpse with dead white face – sandy sleek hair, and a loathsome small straggly beard, and yet is one of the most fascinating men I ever met.'

After the death of her husband in 1914, Nesbit married an engineer called Thomas Tucker. She continued to write children's books and had published 44 novels before her death on 4 May 1924, many of which are still in print today and remain favourite children's stories.

ROBERT LOUIS STEVENSON
(1850–1894)
Scottish novelist, poet and travel writer

Born in Edinburgh to the famous Stevenson family of distinguished lighthouse builders (see chapter V), Robert Louis Stevenson was, as a matter of course, sent to the University of Edinburgh to prepare him for entry into the same profession. Carefree childhood summers spent romping in the open air tempered by winters sitting sedately by the fire nursing his weak lungs left him, at 17, an odd mixture of the hardy and the coddled. Within days of his arrival at Edinburgh, he realised his antipathy for his proposed studies and wrote to his father, Thomas, explaining that he had little or no interest in lighthouse construction. Instead, inspired by Sir Walter Scott and *The Arabian Nights*, his imagination wove wonderful romances around the coast and islands that he had visited with his father, and he wanted to pursue a career as a writer to capture some of these stories on paper.

Thomas Stevenson reluctantly agreed, insisting that Robert Louis finish a law degree first to have something to fall back on, and he passed the examinations for admission to the Bar at 25. On graduation, Stevenson set off to find a climate that would be beneficial to his health, trying various artists' colonies in Fontainebleau, Barbizon, Grez and Nemours and making the journeys described in *An Inland Voyage* (1878) and *Travels with a Donkey* (1879) in the Cevennes.

Soon he had met his future wife – the American Mrs Fanny Vandegrift Osbourne – and surrounded himself with a merry band of friends, including Sidney Colvin, Mrs Sitwell, Andrew Lang and Edmund Gosse. They spent their time visiting galleries and theatres, but Stevenson still had time to write more than 20 articles and essays for magazines. This made his parents' increasingly bitter charges that he was an idler somewhat unfair. The writer did not inform his family when he followed his sick beloved to her San Francisco home in 1879, travelling steerage to save money and arriving near death himself in Monterey. Luckily, he was nursed back to health by some ranchers and later wrote about the experiences in *The Amateur Emigrant* (1895) and *Across the Plains* (1892).

However, ill health and penury dogged him, and in December 1879 in San Francisco, he described himself as 'all alone on forty-five cents a day, and sometimes less'. For the second time that year he found himself close to death, when Mrs Osbourne, newly separated from her husband and recovered from her own illness, nursed him back to health. Fortunately for the writer, when his father heard of his illness he relented and cabled him some money. Stevenson and Mrs Osbourne married in May 1880, though he was 'a mere complication of cough and bones'.

Between 1880 and 1887, Stevenson journeyed widely in England, Scotland and France, trying to improve his health. Despite the burden of his failing lungs, he produced the bulk of his best-known work during this period: *Treasure Island* (1883), *Kidnapped* (1886), *The Strange Case of Dr Jekyll and Mr Hyde* (1886) and *A Child's Garden of Verses* (1885). On the death of his father, in 1887, Stevenson felt free to move to Colorado, but never reached there. After halting temporarily at Saranac Lake in the Adirondacks and beginning *The Master of Ballantrae* (1889), he decided to venture to the South Pacific on a chartered yacht instead.

Wanting to stake a claim in the Pacific, in 1890 he purchased 400 acres of land in Upolu, one of the Samoan Islands, naming his estate Vailima or 'Five Rivers'. An attempt to enter local politics disillusioned him utterly, but he continued to write and *The Ebb Tide* (1893) dates from this period.

For a time during the summer of 1894, Stevenson felt depressed, calling each new attempt at writing 'ditch water' and begging God to release him from his agony. While struggling to open a bottle of wine he suddenly fell to the ground, and died within a few hours, probably of a cerebral haemorrhage. The natives surrounded their Tusitala ('Teller of Tales') with a watch guard, carrying him several miles upon their shoulders to the top of a cliff overlooking the sea, where he was buried.

ABRAHAM (BRAM) STOKER
(1847–1912)
Actor-manager of the Lyceum Theatre
who invented a vampiric alter ego

Bram Stoker started off life as the invalid of his Dublin-based family, unable to walk or stand for periods of time and often confined to bed. As a result, he spent the rest of his life searching for a literary alter ego, which he created most completely in *Dracula* (1897). Indeed, everlasting sleep and the resurrection of the dead, which are the central themes of the book, can be traced back to Stoker's own childhood illness and to long days spent listening to his mother's gruesome tales of the cholera epidemic of 1832.

Determined to shake off the 'weakling' tag, the young Stoker worked hard to build up his physique and conquer his shyness, eventually being named University Athlete at Trinity College, Dublin. His father would not hear of his becoming a writer and, instead, insisted that Stoker take a steady and relatively untaxing job as a clerk at Dublin Castle. With hindsight, it is easy to imagine the torments of the creative Stoker as he worked on the tedious *Duties of Clerks of Petty Sessions in Ireland* (1879).

Stoker continued to write, and his short stories were published by The London Society and in *The Shamrock*. He also undertook various interesting but unpaid positions, such as theatrical editor for Dublin's *Evening Mail* and later, editor of *The Irish Echo*.

On one occasion, the great actor Henry Irving was so pleased with Stoker's review of his production of *Hamlet* that he asked to meet him. As a result, the pair subsequently became close friends and, in 1878, Irving made an offer that would change Stoker's life: the chance to become actor-manager of the Lyceum Theatre in London. Stoker promptly resigned and married an ex-lover of Oscar Wilde's, Florence Balcombe. They married, but she did not settle well into London married life with Stoker. Despite the birth of a baby, Noel, in 1879, the couple were soon estranged.

Stoker kept his post at the Lyceum for 27 years, also acting as devoted factotum to the tyrannical Irving while he wrote *Dracula*. Set in Transylvania and Yorkshire, it was considered extremely shocking at the time with its scenes of female vampiric lust. The constant references to 'purity' and 'tainted blood' may well have been a reference to syphilis, which was claimed by at least one biographer to have been the cause of Stoker's demise.

JULES VERNE
(1828–1905)
Pioneer of science fiction writing
who was deliberately shot by his nephew

It is a myth that as a child Jules Verne stowed away on board a ship bound for Asia, only to be intercepted by his furious father at the first port. Nonetheless, he had a passion for the sea, being brought up in a house in the bustling seaside town of Nantes and with long summers spent in a country house on the Loire.

As a young man Verne set off for Paris vowing to study law, but instead spent his time writing librettos for operas and composing a number of extravagant travellers' tales with carefully prepared scientific and geographical details for the *Musée des Familes*. Though these stories were to reveal the seeds of his true talent, Verne's father was furious and refused all further support, forcing his son to make a living as a stockbroker.

With the help of his wife, Honorine de Viane Morel, and the novelists Alexandre Dumas and Victor Hugo, Verne overcame repeated rejections and joined forces with Pierre-Jules Hetzel, an important influence on his future work. Hetzel, who had edited the works of other authors such as Georges Sand, painstakingly worked to remove the clunkiness and laboured details from Verne's work. In particular, he encouraged Verne to turn sad endings into happy ones, remove political messages and add a touch of comedy to the narrative.

Hits followed thick and fast, from *Journey to the Centre of the Earth* (1864), to *20,000 Leagues Under the Sea* (1869) and *Around the World in Eighty Days* (1872). In all, Verne produced 54 volumes of work, dubbed the 'Extraordinary Voyages'. Their success, and the consequent lucrative theatre rights, enabled him to buy a small ship called the *Saint-Michel*.

However, in 1886, an event occurred which was to haunt Verne for the rest of his life. His nephew, Gaston, of whom he was very fond, fired two shots at him and hit him in the left leg, leaving him with a permanent limp. The deliberate nature of the act could not be denied given the number of shots and Gaston was placed in an asylum for the rest of his life. Although this incident was hushed up, Verne became depressed. Desperate for activities to divert him, he got himself elected as a town councillor of Amiens and served there for 15 years. He died of diabetes while overseeing the publication of his final novels, *Invasion of the Sea* (1905) and *The Lighthouse at the End of the World* (1905). However, he had one last story for the world.

In 1863, he had written a book called *Paris in the Twentieth Century*, about a boy who lives in a world of high-speed trains, glass skyscrapers, gas-powered automobiles, calculators and a worldwide communications network. Hetzel locked up this manuscript in a safe as he felt its black pessimism would damage the author's burgeoning career. It was discovered in 1989 by his great-grandson and published in 1994.

HG WELLS
(1866–1946)
Science fiction writer and social commentator

Herbert George Wells, the son of a tradesman, failed in his first career as a draper. He retrained at grammar school and won a scholarship to the Normal School of Science, where he was taught biology by TH Huxley and developed a lifelong interest in evolution. However, he was uninspired by the teaching he received in the second year, and so in 1887, he left without obtaining a degree.

In 1895 Wells found success, particularly in the US, following the publication of his science fiction story *The Time Machine* (1895). This was followed by two more successful novels, *The Island of Dr Moreau* (1896) and *The War of the Worlds* (1898). *Cosmopolitan* serialised two of his books, and his work also appeared in other magazines.

Around this time Wells also began writing non-fiction books about politics, technology and the future, including *Anticipations of the Reaction of Mechanical and Scientific Progress Upon Human Life and Thought* (1901), *The Discovery of the Future* (1902) and *Mankind in the Making* (1903). These books impressed the leaders of the Fabian Society and he was invited to join. After he failed to persuade the society to mutate into a large pressure group agitating for change, he attempted to gain control of the organisation. Finding little support among his peers, the author resigned from the Fabian Society in 1908, but continued to be politically active, writing the book *A Modern Utopia* (1905), which argued for a society that was run and organised by humanistic and well-educated people.

In his early scientific writings, Wells predicted the invention of modern weapons such as the atomic bomb. As a result, he was horrified by the outbreak of World War I, but felt that the government should take the chance to establish a new world order. He visited Russia during the Bolshevik Revolution and spoke with Lenin and Trotsky about how their new country should be run, expanding his theme in the book *The Outline of History* (1920).

In the 1920s and 1930s, Wells, by now an international figure, argued that society needed world government and was a vocal supporter of the League of Nations. He also argued that, if education was the key to world order, it was natural that societies should be ruled by the intelligentsia as outlined in his novel, *The Shape of Things to Come* (1933). He died on 13 August 1946, while working on a project that dealt with the dangers of nuclear war.

CHAPTER IX

❧

GREASEPAINT MONKEYS,
NE'ER DO WELLS & THE HOI POLLOI

JACK BLACK
(*fl.* 1860)
Queen Victoria's rat catcher

Jack Black, one of the low-life characters immortalised in Henry Mayhew's monumental *London Labour and the London Poor*, was renowned during the 1850s as the capital's most efficient exterminator of vermin – he distributed handbills proclaiming himself 'Rat and Mole Destroyer to Her Majesty'. A rat catcher from childhood, Black's principal income came from supplying live animals to publicans, who then organised 'rat matches' in which their patrons' dogs killed the animals by the dozen in special pits built in the cellars of the pubs. Catchers were paid three pence for each rat, and one London landlord used to purchase 26,000 a year.

Catching rats was a risky job, and the principal danger was infection from the bite of a sewer rat. 'When the bite is a bad one,' Black told Mayhew, 'it festers and forms a hard core in the ulcer, which throbs very much indeed. This core is as big as a boiled fish's eye, and as hard as stone. I generally cuts the bite out clean with a lancet and squeezes... I've been bitten nearly everywhere, even where I can't name to you, sir.'

Black's skills, Mayhew noted, extended far beyond the capture of rats and moles. He also stuffed animals and birds, trained fish and caught fish (with his bare hands) for fishmongers and aquariums.

WILLIAM CROCKFORD
(1775–1844)
Fishmonger-turned-gambler who beggared half the aristocratic families of England

During the early Victorian age, London was awash with bored young aristocrats who, having little to do during a period of protracted peace, assuaged their tedium by gambling. By far the most opulent and popular of the various gaming 'hells' that opened to cater to these appetites was William Crockford's Club. Established just off Pall Mall in 1828, it was run by Crockford, a former fishmonger from the East End whose extraordinary skill at odds-making had already earned him a fortune said to be well in excess of £50,000. For all his success, Crockford never outgrew his lowly roots, and was careful not to imply he was in any sense the equal of his patrons, particularly when they owed him money.

Crockford's Club, nonetheless, numbered among its members well over a thousand of the richest men in England and offered several different games of chance, notably the popular dice game Hazard. The club was socially exclusive – with a membership committee chaired by the Duke of Wellington – and a congenial meeting place even for those who disdained gambling. Crockford's chef was Eustache Ude, then generally regarded as the finest cook in Europe.

Another reason for Crockford's uncanny success was his encyclopaedic knowledge of the expectations of the heirs to Britain's principal aristocratic fortunes. It was widely believed that the former fishmonger knew, to the pound and to the hour, exactly when prospective members would come into their inheritances, and could thus arrange to extend suitably timed invitations to visit his luxurious premises to the heirs of every major family. In the course of 15 years of furious gambling, Crockford won hundreds of thousands of pounds from a generation of hapless young aristocrats – indeed there are still eminent families in Britain today whose fortunes have never recovered from their ancestors' encounters with him.

Despite his success, Crockford nonetheless came to a bad end, investing money and all his hopes on a young colt he had entered in the Derby of 1844. Sadly for him, this proved to be the most crooked horse race ever run – one syndicate substituted the favourite for another horse; another doped the second favourite; at least one of the principal jockeys was bribed; and a third well-backed horse was older than was claimed and hence stronger than the remainder of the field. Crockford's horse came nowhere in the race and the aged gambler died three days later.

TOM DUDLEY
(1853–1900)
Shipwrecked yacht captain prosecuted for eating his cabin boy

Few legal cases of the Victorian era are better remembered than that of
Regina versus Dudley & Stephens (1884), which helped to establish the
defence of necessity in murder trials.

Tom Dudley, the hapless protagonist in this celebrated trial, was born in
the Essex village of Tollesbury. On the death of his mother, when he was
aged just nine, he went to sea, eventually gaining some renown as a yacht
captain. In 1884, he was engaged to skipper the *Mignonette*, a small yacht
sailing out to Australia. Dudley hired a navigator, Edwin Stephens, as his
mate, and the small crew was completed by an ordinary seaman named
Edmund Brooks and cabin boy Richard Parker, 17. The four sailed from
England in May of that year.

Less than two months later the *Mignonette* foundered in moderate seas off
the Cape of Good Hope, forcing the crew to abandon ship in their lifeboat.
Equipped with only two tins of turnips and no water, they drifted for nearly
three weeks – by which time all were starving and tormented by thirst.

On the twentieth day, Parker was killed by Dudley, who stabbed him in the
jugular vein while Stephens held him down. All three surviving crew members
then drank the boy's blood and consumed 'quite half' of his body. Brooks
commented: 'We partook of it with quite as much relish as ordinary food.'
Sustained in this way, the three seamen were eventually rescued and returned
to England, where, having candidly explained how they survived, captain and
mate were both arrested. The ensuing court case aroused great controversy, the
trial hinging largely on whether the choice of the victim was random. Some of
Dudley's accounts reported that all four men had agreed to draw lots to select
one of their number for death, but the prosecution responded that the lottery, if
it had ever taken place, had been rigged; Parker was chosen because eating the
ship's cabin boy was an established 'custom of the sea'.

Judges who debated the case concluded that acquitting Dudley and
Stephens would set a dangerous precedent by making murder legal in certain

extreme circumstances. The two sailors were accordingly found guilty and sentenced to death, but both were immediately reprieved by Queen Victoria, and their sentences commuted to a mere six months' imprisonment. This verdict did, in effect, establish the defence of necessity, while retaining the prerogative of mercy for the Crown.

Although the sailors enjoyed popular support, they were inevitably objects of curiosity and Dudley emigrated to Australia upon his release. He became a tent-maker, but died in 1900, aged 46, of bubonic plague.

AMELIA DYER
(1839–1896)
Infamous murderess and baby farmer

The practice of baby farming was one of the great scandals of the Victorian age. Poor families, burdened by yet another child they could scarcely afford, would hand the baby over to a 'farmer', usually a middle-aged woman, who agreed, in exchange for a substantial one-off fee and suitable clothing, to bring it up as her own. Successful baby farmers might take responsibility for half a dozen infants or more, but the costs were considerable and several of the women who practised the art found it more expedient to dispose of their helpless charges and pocket the fee. The most notorious case was that of Amelia Dyer, 'the Reading baby farmer' – she was convicted of seven murders.

Dyer appeared in Reading, Berkshire, in 1895 and placed newspaper advertisements offering to adopt and board young children. In March 1896, a boatman recovered the body of a baby girl, Helena Fry, wrapped in brown paper, from the River Thames. A subsequent dragging of the river revealed two more grizzly parcels. A faint address on one of the packages led the police to Dyer, a former member of the Salvation Army who had moved about constantly and changed her name in an attempt to evade the authorities. Dyer confessed, telling police they would be able to identify her victims because she had killed each baby in an identical manner, strangling them with white tape, which she left wrapped tight around the infants' necks. A large pile of baby clothes and letters from anxious mothers were discovered in her home.

She was tried, found guilty and hanged at Newgate Prison. The scandal surrounding this and similar cases led to a revision of the legislation relating to the adoption of infants.

PABLO FANQUE
(1796–1871)
Britain's first black circus owner, immortalised by John Lennon

Pablo Fanque – born William Darby, in Norwich, in 1796 – was one of the most celebrated and successful British circus proprietors of the Victorian age. The son of a butler who was probably a freed slave, Fanque was orphaned while still a child and was apprenticed to William Batty, the owner of a travelling show. In time, the boy picked up numerous acrobatic skills and also trained with renowned circus owner Andrew Ducrow. By the mid-1830s, he was seen as a first-rate equestrian, acrobat, tightrope walker and trainer of show horses, and billed in the press as 'the loftiest jumper in England'.

In 1841 Fanque left Batty's show and opened his own with just two horses. He performed mostly in the North of England and gradually developed a fully-fledged circus that included clowns and acrobatic acts. By the late 1840s, the Fanque Circus Royal was one of the best known in the country, but the proprietor's private life was tinged with tragedy. His wife, Susannah, died in 1848, the result of a freak accident at a show – she was struck on the head by several heavy planks when part of the wooden banks of seating collapsed.

Fanque continued to run his circus after his wife's death and was joined by his children. He seems to have encountered little racism in the course of his career – the chaplain of the Showman's Guild remarked: 'In the great brotherhood of the equestrian world there is no colour line, for, although Pablo

Fanque was of African extraction, he speedily made his way to the top of his profession. The camaraderie of the Ring has but one test, ability.'

Pablo Fanque died in Stockport in 1871. Nearly a century later, John Lennon found an old playbill advertising a benefit performance for one of his circus's stars that had been held in Rotherham in 1843. Lennon adapted the wording on the poster to write the lyrics of 'Being for the Benefit of Mr Kite', a song on The Beatles' album *Sgt Pepper's Lonely Hearts Club Band*.

CHARLES AUGUSTUS HOWELL
(1840–1890)
Society blackmailer

Charles Augustus Howell became notorious during the middle years of Queen Victoria's reign as a cunning and successful blackmailer of socially prominent men. Among his victims were Algernon Swinburne, the homosexual poet, and the painter Dante Gabriel Rossetti.

Howell's involvement with Rossetti was one of his most extraordinary adventures. The painter's wife, Elizabeth, had died in 1862 after taking an overdose of laudanum, and the grief-stricken artist had buried a packet of his unpublished manuscripts with her. Seven years later, Rossetti suddenly decided to recover the documents, and prevailed upon his good friend Howell to exhume the body. Howell succeeded in recovering the papers, but then extorted a considerable sum from his acquaintance by threatening to reveal Rossetti's role in the scandalous exhumation. He then compounded matters by forging and selling several examples of the painter's work.

Howell's usual methods were rather more subtle. A favourite device was to enter into a correspondence with a prominent figure and gradually steer the subject of the letters around to a common interest in a sexual perversion or some embarrassing personal inadequacy, pretending to share their interest or problem. He would paste any incriminating responses into a scrapbook and then write to his correspondent regretting that, pressed for money, he had been forced to pawn the book. Failure to supply the large sum required to redeem this item, it was hinted, would lead the pawnbroker to seek a buyer for the letters, which inevitably risked being made public. The blackmailer was successful in obtaining considerable sums from Swinburne in this manner, having presented himself as a fellow fan of *le vice Anglais* and been taken by the poet to several homosexual brothels that specialised in flagellation.

Howell died in 1890, reportedly at the hands of an angry victim who left his body in Glasshouse Street, London, with his throat cut and a half-sovereign placed between his teeth: a traditional punishment for blackmailers. Howell attained posthumous fame of a sort when Arthur Conan Doyle made him the model for the slippery blackmailer in the Sherlock Holmes story, *The Adventure of Charles Augustus Milverton*.

JACK THE RIPPER
(*fl.* 1888)
Serial killer of Whitechapel prostitutes

No one knew who Jack the Ripper was during the Victorian period, and his true identity remains a mystery today. He was not only the most talked-about Victorian criminal, but arguably the most influential. The killer struck five times – perhaps more – in the Whitechapel area in 1888. All of his victims were prostitutes, and each, with a single exception, was more horribly mutilated than the last. The first woman murdered by Jack the Ripper had her throat cut and two incisions made in her abdomen; the last was butchered horribly.

Much of the Ripper's notoriety rests with his evasion of justice. The murderer was never caught and expert opinion remains divided as to whether he died soon after his final murder or escaped the scene and perhaps killed again elsewhere. Numerous theories regarding his identity have been put forward, the most sensational suggesting that he was a member of the royal family or a Freemason killing according to the demands of ritual.

Jack the Ripper's true significance, however, lies in the legacy he left to the East End of London. Press coverage of the murders drew public attention to the shocking conditions that prevailed in Whitechapel and led to considerable pressure for social reform. As the playwright George Bernard Shaw put it in a letter published by the *London Star* shortly before the Ripper's final killing: 'While we Social Democrats were wasting our time on education, agitation and organisation, some independent genius has taken the matter in hand, and by simply murdering and disembowelling four women, converted the proprietary press to an inept sort of Communism.'

LILLIE LANGTRY
(1853–1929)
Actress and mistress of the Prince of Wales

P erhaps the archetypal example of a small-town girl drawn to the big city, Lillie Langtry was born on the Channel Island of Jersey and went to London to make good. Langtry was not, by Victorian standards, a virtuous woman. Her only daughter was certainly not fathered by her husband and may even have been the child of Prince Louis of Battenberg, and her career on the stage was prompted by the looming threat of bankruptcy.

But her extraordinary beauty made her a star and she seems to have moved comfortably in the most elevated social circles, eventually, in 1877, becoming the mistress of Edward, Prince of Wales.

Edward was captivated by Langtry's independence and intelligence – she was one of the few women not to seem overawed by him – and moved decisively to separate her from her unfortunate husband, who suddenly found himself deluged with invitations from various of the prince's friends to sailing and shooting excursions in the distant Highlands. In his absence, Edward installed Langtry as his more-or-less openly acknowledged mistress. When her affair with Edward cooled – quite literally, as she was reputed to have tipped ice down his back as a joke and refused to apologise

– Langtry took to the stage, eventually moving to the United States, where she became a Californian wine maker and published a remarkably discreet autobiography.

Langtry was widowed in 1897 and remarried, two years later, to Hugo de Bathe, a racehorse owner.

DAN LENO
(1860–1904)
The pantomime dame's pantomime dame

Possibly the only world-champion clog dancer to become a friend to royalty, Dan Leno was born into a show business family and became one of the greatest stars of the Victorian music hall. As a pantomime artiste, he displayed such rare subtlety and merit that he was able to make audiences cry just as easily as he made them laugh. Modern dames still employ many of the nuances of character that Leno introduced.

Born in London as George Galvin, Leno made his stage debut at a young age, billed as 'Little George, the Infant Wonder, Contortionist and Posturer'. For years he made a living as an exceptional competitive clog dancer. When the clog's appeal dimmed, he turned to comedy, an art he helped to transform. As a comic, Leno worked alone, a tiny figure in the centre of a big stage, and his humour – focusing on the travails of the lower middle class – was laced with pathos. He was a master of timing and one of the first comedians to place more stress on his 'patter' than on the comic songs that were a staple of the art at the time. His style of closely observed comedy, peppered with awful puns, remained predominant until the advent of 'gag-tellers' in the 1930s.

Leno was the first music hall star to give a command performance for royalty, and appeared frequently at private parties held at Sandringham. He died insane, at the height of his fame, the victim of a crippling nervous illness.

WILLIAM MACREADY
(1793–1873)
Actor whose Macbeth resulted in the deaths of 23 New Yorkers

Arguably the most popular classical actor of Queen Victoria's reign, William Macready is best remembered for a childish feud with an American rival that led to one of the worst riots in the history of New York City. Macready was born into a theatrical family and made his debut in 1816, modelling himself on the posturing Edmund Kean, who was probably the best-known actor of the Regency period. His most successful early roles were those of Rob Roy and William Tell, and by the time his career reached its apogee in the late 1840s, Macready was well-known throughout Britain. He was particularly celebrated for his appearances in Shakespeare's histories and tragedies at the Drury Lane and Covent Garden theatres, playing Macbeth, Henry V and Richard III with equal success.

Macready made several successful tours of America, but in 1843 he became embroiled in a rivalry with the New York actor Edwin Forrest, who accused him of hissing during a performance that the American gave in London. Their rivalry was renewed during Macready's next trip to the US, which was marked by outbursts of anti-English sentiment. A series of disturbances culminated in the assembly of an Irish-American mob estimated at 15,000 outside the Astor Place Opera House just as the curtain went up on Macready's *Macbeth*.

Angry members of the crowd tore down iron railings to use as missiles and bombarded the theatre before riddling the locked doors of the opera house with bullets. The police, despairing of controlling the rioters, called out troops to disperse the crowd. The soldiers, alarmed by the mob's mood, formed ranks and opened fire, resulting in the deaths of 23 men and women; 100 more were badly injured. Macready escaped the opera house through a side door and fled the city in disguise, never to return.

Although he continued to be acclaimed on the English stage, the actor retired to Cheltenham in 1851.

WILLIAM S GILBERT AND ARTHUR SULLIVAN
(1836–1911 and 1842–1900)
Creators of the world's best-loved popular comic operas

William S Gilbert and Arthur Sullivan were the twin giants of popular music in the 19th century, producing a series of short, witty and tuneful operettas that were smash hits on both sides of the Atlantic.

Among their 14 joint compositions were *HMS Pinafore*, *The Pirates of Penzance* and *The Mikado*, most of which were first produced at London's famous Savoy Theatre. *The Mikado*, in particular, provided the template for many of the great musicals of the 20th century, and, all in all, the two figures collaborated for 25 years, although their friendship was rarely harmonious. They were knighted separately (Gilbert no fewer than 24 years after his partner), their characters were very different, and Sullivan, who composed the music, felt increasingly that his gifts were being frittered away in light opera while he aspired to loftier things. But acclaim and money kept the partnership more or less intact until 1896, when their final production, *The Grand Duke*, proved a disastrous failure.

Sullivan died of pneumonia four years later and his wish to be buried in the family plot in Bromley was thwarted by Queen Victoria, who ordered he be interred in St Paul's Cathedral instead. Gilbert followed a decade later in somewhat peculiar circumstances. He was giving two young girls a swimming lesson and, when one found herself in difficulty, the elderly librettist dived in to save her and suffered a fatal heart attack.

CHAPTER X

MAKERS OF MUSIC

FREDERICK DELIUS
(1862–1934)
Composer, orange-planter, Yorkshireman

Frederick Delius, who spent many of his most productive years in
France, was a composer of talent who was born in Bradford and
whose earliest musical training came via a spell spent working as an
orange-planter in Jacksonville, Florida. Born to German parents who had
moved to Yorkshire to find employment in the cotton trade, 'Fritz' Delius
felt little attraction for his adopted homeland and was at his happiest
in Paris, where he moved after his American sojourn, and where he
contracted the venereal disease syphilis.

His parents, supportive of his desire to become a professional
musician, later enrolled him at the Leipzig Conservatorium, where in
the late 1880s he met the Norwegian composer Edvard Grieg, who
would become both a mentor and a lifelong friend.

On returning to Paris, Delius began composing orchestral works.
He drew on an unusually eclectic range of influences, from English,
Norwegian and German folk songs to American Indian music
and Negro spirituals; his works, characterised by lush harmonies,
were performed chiefly in Germany until Sir Thomas Beecham, the
English conductor, impresario and modernist, began to promote them
in Britain.

Delius's masterpiece – the opera *A Village Romeo and Juliet* – was
composed in 1901, at the very end of the Victorian period. The decade
that followed witnessed his development as a musician, with the
completion of *Sea Drift*, a setting that encapsulates his nostalgia for
lost love.

By the early 1920s, Delius had been rendered blind and quadriplegic
by syphilis, although his speech and his mind remained unimpaired. All
his later works were composed through an amanuensis, a youthful fellow
Yorkshireman by the name of Eric Fenby, whose initial introduction to
the great man came in the form of a fan letter.

EDWARD ELGAR
(1857–1934)
Composer who wrote 'Land of Hope and Glory'

Although remembered today pre-eminently as the composer of the 'Pomp and Circumstance March No 1', better known as 'Land of Hope and Glory', Edward Elgar was a musician of melodic genius who also composed the *Enigma Variations* and *The Dream of Gerontius*.

The son of a piano tuner and dealer in instruments and scores, Elgar grew up in the countryside outside Worcester surrounded by music. 'There is,' he once remarked, 'music in the air, music all around us, the world is full of it and you simply take as much as you require.' From unpromising beginnings – his first job was as bandmaster of a lunatic asylum, and he also worked as conductor of the Worcester Glee Club – Elgar rose to great heights, ending his career as Master of the King's Music. One early coup was his marriage, to the daughter of a major general nine years his senior and several degrees his social superior; another was playing at a Birmingham Festival, under the baton of Antonín Dvořák. Elgar's first major orchestral work, popularly known as the *Enigma Variations*, received its premiere in 1899.

Elgar's other works include two symphonies, a cello concerto and some music for brass bands. He died in 1934, from a malignant tumour.

ROBERT HOPE-JONES
(1859–1914)
Organ-builder whose unappreciated work led to the creation
of the Mighty Wurlitzer

Wurlitzer organs could never have risen through the floors of silent movie 'picture palaces', and church organs would lack the formidable array of stops enabling a single person to imitate entire orchestras, had it not been for the pioneering work of Robert Hope-Jones, one of the greatest, if least-remembered, musical mavericks of the 19th century.

Hope-Jones was born on the Wirral, close to Chester. He displayed a scientific leaning while at school and found employment as an engineer with a telephone company. There, his work on low-voltage circuits led him to consider the application of electrical power to musical instruments – most notably the organ. He proceeded to revolutionise the organ by connecting the keyboard to the air valves electrically, rather than depending on the clumsy mechanical valves that had been employed previously. He also added consoles full of extra stops that gave the instrument the power to change its range and tone in imitation of everything from violins to cymbals.

Hope-Jones's theories required him to make considerable technical innovations. His organs 'spoke' at much higher frequencies than their predecessors so they could better imitate other instruments. They earned him some acclaim in his native Britain and he set up factories in Battersea and Norwich, before leaving the country for the United States, aged 44.

The cause of Hope-Jones's departure is unclear; some sources say he was threatened with some kind of prosecution, others that he fled the threats of rival organ-builders and parishioners angered by his efforts to replace their beloved church organs with his newfangled apparatus. In any event, the inventor recommenced his work in New York State, where his investors in a new factory included Mark Twain, who made a profit of $100,000 on the venture.

Hope-Jones built nearly 40 organs in the US, and won the contract to install one of his machines in the prestigious Carnegie Hall. The experiment proved a disaster, however, with Andrew Carnegie himself dismissing the Hope-Jones organ (which not only included drum effects, but also lightning and storm machines as well) as being more suited to a bawdy house than a concert hall.

Lapsing into depression, Hope-Jones watched listlessly as his venture slumped into financial ruin. His wife left him and he was forced to sell his patents and name to Wurlitzer, the organ company. It used them to begin manufacture of the vast, and still-celebrated, quasi-orchestral monstrosities that it sold by the hundreds to cinemas looking for a cost-effective accompaniment to the silent movies of the early 20th century.

Hope-Jones committed suicide in 1914, just before the American craze for his organs took off, by gassing himself. The method chosen was ingenious. Instead of using just one outlet tube, Hope-Jones fitted two to the gas tap, stuffing one into his mouth and lighting the other to disguise the smell of escaping vapour. Even in death he remained an innovator.

JENNY LIND
(1820–1887)
'Swedish Nightingale' admired by Queen Victoria

No opera singer of the 19th century, not even Nellie Melba, surpassed Johanna Maria Lind – Jenny Lind as she was better known – in renown. The Swedish star, born in Stockholm, became famous for her technical agility and for the purity of her voice.

Although the earliest years of her career were spent in Sweden, where she made her debut in 1838, Lind owed much of her early fame to Queen Victoria, who was impressed by a performance that she heard in Dresden. Word of the queen's admiration spread, and Lind came to London in 1847 to deliver a recital that caused a sensation. This was followed by acclaimed appearances in Norwich, Manchester and Liverpool.

The soprano – who received vocal training in France from the Spanish teacher Manuel Garcia – was nominally an opera singer, but had only limited acting ability. She returned to the European concert circuit in triumph in the late 1840s, and in 1850 crossed the Atlantic, touring the eastern seaboard of the United States and earning the soubriquet 'The Swedish Nightingale'. The price of tickets on this tour reached unheard-of heights, thanks largely to her canny manager, the brilliant flimflammer PT Barnum. Lind's talent, looks and fame attracted numerous admirers. She received a proposal from Hans Christian Andersen, which she rejected, marrying the pianist Otto Goldschmidt instead in 1851; he had been a pupil of Felix Mendelssohn and later became her accompanist.

Lind performed only rarely after her marriage, generally in support of charitable causes, and spent almost all of her later life in London. She dispersed much of the fortune she had earned in support of various philanthropic causes, but she found time to work for several years as a professor of singing at the Royal College of Music during the early 1880s. Lind's final years were spent in Great Malvern, Worcestershire, where she is buried in the town cemetery.

FRANZ LISZT
(1811–1886)
Composer and piano virtuoso

The supreme piano virtuoso of the century, Franz Liszt was also one of the most progressive conductors and composers of his day. He devoted himself to the promotion of new music from the likes of Richard Wagner and Hector Berlioz, but was equally innovative as a composer, although his work in this field was only truly recognised after his death.

Born in Hungary, Liszt was educated in Vienna, where he met Ludwig van Beethoven and studied composition under Wolfgang Amadeus Mozart's old rival Antonio Salieri. In 1823 he and his family moved to Paris, where the boy gained such renown as a child prodigy at the piano that he was invited to make three visits to Britain between 1824 and 1827. An unhappy love affair and the death of his father temporarily halted Liszt's rise, but the French Revolution of 1830 revived him, and an encounter with Nicolò Paganini inspired him to attempt for the piano what Paganini had achieved with the violin.

By the 1840s, Liszt was recognised as the pre-eminent pianist of the day and he became renowned for his generosity, funding the studies of many students and teaching at least 400 of them for free. Liszt toured Europe repeatedly, inspiring bouts of what became known as 'Lisztomania' wherever he went. He also established a fashion for solo recitals that endures to this day. It was not until 1848 that, feeling drained by continual touring, he settled in the German town of Weimar and devoted himself to composing.

His private life was at times scandalous. In 1835 he ran away from Paris with the wife of the Count d'Agoult, fleeing with her to Geneva and fathering three children by her. Fifteen years later the great musician fell in love with a married princess, Carolyne zu Sayn-Wittgenstein, who became his lover and whom he was only prevented from marrying by intrigues in the Vatican. Friends were surprised, given Liszt's love life, when he developed a religious inclination, taking minor orders and having himself tonsured in 1865.

Liszt's fame as a pianist seldom translated to acclaim for his abilities as a composer; his works were regarded as too 'showy', and it was not until a final visit to Britain in 1886 that his more technically challenging pieces were at last greeted with genuine enthusiasm. He died of pneumonia in Bayreuth later that same year.

FELIX MENDELSSOHN
(1809–1847)
Well-travelled German whose most celebrated work was inspired
by a visit to the Hebrides

Work consumed the life of the German composer Felix Mendelssohn. He began working at 5am and was known for packing more invention into his compositions than his contemporaries. As early as 1825, the Italian composer Luigi Cherubini warned that 'he puts too much material into his coat', but nonetheless Mendelssohn's *Octet for Strings*, composed later that same year, displayed such a wealth of ideas that it has been described as 'perhaps the most astonishing example of youthful genius in all Western music'.

Mendelssohn was born in Hamburg but travelled widely, making a total of 10 visits to Britain in his short lifetime. His compositions, which included the overture *The Hebrides* (better known as 'Fingal's Cave'), were lush and romantic. They also divided opinion in his day – he was both renowned for his technique and laughed at for his sentimentality. Mendelssohn's tours of Britain and his familiarity with all things British inspired several other important compositions, including incidental music for *A Midsummer Night's Dream* and *A Scottish Symphony*, but the composer's latter years were passed in Germany, where he founded an Academy of Arts in Berlin and a music academy in Leipzig.

Mendelssohn died of a cerebral haemorrhage just as a contemporary, Richard Wagner, was just about to take classical music in new and even more dramatic directions. Dismissed by many as a mere sentimentalist, Mendelssohn's reputation suffered as a consequence. Wagner himself dismissed his rival's conducting with the comment that it left him 'peering into a very abyss of superficiality, an utter void'.

ROBERT NEWMAN
(1858–1926)
Impresario who created the Proms

Born into a wealthy family and trained as a singer in Italy, Robert Newman embarked on a career as an impresario of classical music, but soon despaired of educating a more or less philistine British public to share his own elevated musical tastes. Newman's solution to this problem was what became the institution of the Promenade Concerts, the first of which he organised in London in 1895. 'I am going to run nightly concerts,' he told his conductor, Henry Wood, 'and train the public by easy stages. Popular at first, gradually raising the standard until I have created a public for classical and modern music.'

The impresario had prior experience managing promenades (concerts at which patrons were free to eat, drink, smoke and stroll around the auditorium) at the chosen venue, the Queen's Hall in Regent Street, and his inaugural season was an immediate success. The early Proms were lengthy affairs by modern standards, lasting up to three hours each, but the essential pattern established by Newman has been followed to this day. Programmes featured popular classics, interspersed with occasional performances of more serious pieces, all performed by a resident orchestra and made available to the public at the lowest possible price – in 1895 a season ticket cost one guinea.

The first season of Proms consisted of 10 concerts, and the total number of performances was expanded as the years went by. Newman's particular innovation was the 'Grand Fantasia', a medley of popular highlights from opera occupying the second half of a concert.

The series was presented under the banner of 'Mr Robert Newman's Promenade Concerts' until 1915, when – Newman having run into financial troubles – the Queen's Hall lease and the Proms themselves were taken over by the music publisher Chappell & Co. Newman nonetheless remained involved in the presentation of the concerts until his death in 1926.

HUBERT PARRY
(1848–1918)
Director of the Royal College of Music and composer of 'Jerusalem'

A Romantic composer, inspired by Johann Sebastian Bach and Johannes Brahms, Hubert Parry – in the opinion of many critics – brought a distinctly British sensibility to music for the first time since the days of Henry Purcell two centuries earlier. His potent diatonic style heavily influenced contemporaries, such as Edward Elgar, and his pupils, including Ralph Vaughan Williams and Gustav Holst.

Parry came from a good family and was educated at Eton and Oxford. He displayed musical talent at an early age and earned a degree in music while still at school. However, it was not until he fell under the influence of Edward Dannreuther, the pre-eminent British music teacher of the mid-19th century, that he found his true voice. By the late 1870s, Parry's early chamber music was being widely performed, not least at recitals given at Dannreuther's home. Later in life he became still more renowned for his choral works.

As a composer, Parry proved himself a musician of considerable range, writing symphonies, oratorios, concertos, opera and miscellaneous works for the orchestra, even though his development is generally agreed to have been hampered by the vast administrative burden he shouldered as a lecturer at, and later principal of, the Royal College of Music. As a man, he was regarded as an inspiring teacher who employed considerable personal charm to deliver, in the words of Holst, 'a vision rather than a lecture'.

Parry's most celebrated work was the setting he composed for William Blake's poem 'Jerusalem' in 1916; the hymn has become an alternative English national anthem.

CHARLES STANFORD
(1852–1924)
Conductor, teacher and composer

Few British musicians have taught a list of pupils as illustrious as that of Charles Stanford, an Irishman who combined the posts of professor of music at Cambridge University and professor of composition at the Royal College of Music. Originally a cellist, Stanford attended Queens' College, Cambridge, as an organ scholar and took up conducting while there. He served as organist of Trinity College for nearly two decades and began composing – mostly operas – in the late 1870s.

Today, Stanford's renown rests largely on his church music, written mainly for the organ, but in his day he was best known for performing choral works at various provincial music festivals. The composer's musical feuds, including a notoriously acrimonious disagreement with Edward Elgar, were interspersed with extensive teaching duties. His pupils included 20th-century composers Gustav Holst, Ralph Vaughan Williams and Herbert Howells.

Stanford was knighted in 1902 and, on his death 22 years later, was buried next to Henry Purcell in Westminster Abbey.

RICHARD WAGNER
(1813–1883)
Composer, nationalist, anti-Semite

Wilhelm Richard Wagner, indisputably one of the greatest composers of the 19th century, wrote some of the most dramatic and ambitious operas ever composed, but, in Britain at least, rarely escaped criticism for his German nationalism and anti-Semitism.

Born in the same year as his Italian counterpart, Giuseppe Verdi, Wagner was raised in a chaotic environment, his supposed father – there is considerable doubt concerning his paternity – died when he was only six months old. Musically self-taught until his arrival at the University of Leipzig, aged 18, Wagner grew into a supreme egoist with so firm a belief in his own genius that he took to living well beyond his means.

As a composer, Wagner was particularly well noted for writing his own librettos, for his elaborate leitmotifs (recurring themes) and for his mastership of contrapuntal texture. The German believed firmly that music should incorporate the arts of poetry, song, dance and stagecraft, a concept lying at the heart of the 16-hour, four-opera *Ring Cycle* that remains his most celebrated work.

The composer's private life was rarely happy. He grew to detest his first wife, Minna Planer, who was unfaithful to him only a few months after their marriage and later lapsed into acute depression. He soon embarked on a long series of barely disguised affairs. His involvement with a German nationalist movement forced him to endure more than a decade of exile; and his finances were so disordered that by 1864, he had exhausted his credit and faced debtors' prison. Wagner's position was saved only by the intervention of Ludwig II, King of Bavaria, who became his patron and settled him in Munich. While there, the composer fell in love with the wife of the conductor Hans von Bülow (who was also the daughter of Franz Liszt), began another affair, and eventually married her.

Wagner lived a peripatetic life and paid three visits to London. The first, in 1839, came when he fled Latvia, leaving behind some enormous debts – the stormy sea voyage he and Minna endured becoming the inspiration for *The Flying Dutchman*. His second visit, in 1855, came when the composer was still short of cash and needed to pick up some instant income from a series of concerts. The third, 22 years later, took place at the height of his fame and it was on this occasion that Wagner's vociferous anti-Semitism was criticised by the press.

CHAPTER XI

ARTISTIC VISIONARIES

AUBREY BEARDSLEY
(1872–1898)
Artist, aesthete and erotophile

The versatile Aubrey Beardsley (who was an able caricaturist as well as an illustrator, and whose relatives claimed he was a better musician than an artist) had a short but scandalous career towards the end of the Victorian age.

Beardsley was born into genteel poverty in Brighton; his mother provided most of the family's income by giving piano lessons. Ill from the age of six with tuberculosis, he struggled to hold down a job as he got older, but displayed precocious talent as an artist of exquisite economy, working in the Art Nouveau style. Bored by his job as a clerk, and aged only 19, he plucked up the courage to show his work to one of the leading Pre-Raphaelites, Edward Burne-Jones, who told him: 'I seldom or never advise anyone to take up art as a profession, but in your case I can do nothing else.' Burne-Jones arranged for him to receive training at the Westminster School of Art.

Beardsley soon attracted the attention of publishers, contributing 300 drawings to a new edition of Sir Thomas Malory's *Le Morte d'Arthur* and contributing regularly to *The Yellow Book*, then the principal publication of the 'decadents' of the Aesthetic movement. It was through this that Beardsley met Oscar Wilde, whose salacious *Salomé* he illustrated in a Japanese-influenced style. Beardsley's libidinous pictures, drawn in stark black and white, aroused considerable controversy; even the artist himself became troubled by his more outrageous work. In a fit of religious-inspired guilt shortly before his death, he begged his publisher – the notorious pornographer Leonard Smithers – to withdraw the most explicit from publication.

Those who didn't know Aubrey Beardsley assumed he was a libertine. Those who did know him asserted that he was a boy who had scarcely grown up. In any case, he loved to shock with his Sadean scenes of debauchery: half-clothed women and Satyr-like men sporting gigantic phalluses.

By the time he reached his mid-20s, Beardsley knew that he was dying, and moved to the south of France in search of a more tolerable climate.

Increasingly incapacitated, he found drawing difficult and was forced to switch from pen and ink to pencil. His final moments, it appears, were spent drawing; his favourite gold pen was found embedded nib-first in the floorboards beneath his body, where it had fallen when he died. After he died, even the *Catholic Encyclopaedia* was moved to say of him: 'He carried the art of black and white further than any man since Albrecht Dürer.'

Beardsley's biographers have speculated, without providing any firm evidence, that the close relationship he enjoyed with his phenomenally clever actress sister, Mabel, was incestuous. However, all that can be said with certainty is that the two shared a home, Mabel miscarried a child by an unknown father in 1892, and that she was the chief beneficiary of Beardsley's will.

EDWARD BURNE-JONES
(1833–1898)
Painter and promoter of stained glass

For a man once intent on entering the priesthood, Edward Burne-Jones certainly led a remarkably bohemian life, touring Italy with John Ruskin, promoting the scandalous Pre-Raphaelites, and sharing a London room with a friend, William Morris, who fell in love with Burne-Jones's wife. The artist's early life was touched by tragedy. His mother died six days after he was born and his father was forced to have the boy raised by a housekeeper who lacked much maternal feeling. Nonetheless, Burne-Jones was a success at school and won a place to study at Oxford, where he planned to work towards ordination.

Having decided, with the encouragement of his Oxford friend John Ruskin, to embark instead on an artistic career, Burne-Jones became heavily involved in the mid-Victorian revival of stained-glass window-making. As well as jewellery and tapestry, he was a painter and illustrator, preparing plates for an acclaimed new edition of *Chaucer* for William Morris's Kelmscott Press, and experimenting with some novel linear compositions. Barely appreciated early on, Burne-Jones's reputation slowly grew from the late 1870s and he emerged as a hero of the Aesthetic movement, several of whom – notably Aubrey Beardsley – he actively encouraged.

His private life was occasionally tumultuous. While living in Fulham, his wife Georgiana became the object of William Morris's unrequited affections. Burne-Jones engaged in a passionate affair with a Greek model named Maria Zambaco, who sensationally attempted suicide in public when he ended their relationship. He survived the scandal and eventually became firmly embedded in the establishment. He was made a baronet in 1894, became an associate of the Royal Academy and was uncle to both Rudyard Kipling and a future prime minister, Stanley Baldwin.

EDWIN LANDSEER
(1802–1873)
Painter whose best-known work was Monarch of the Glen

Edwin Landseer was the foremost painter of animals in the Victorian era and, in the opinion of many of his contemporaries, the greatest since Stubbs. Given the fervour with which the Victorians regarded their animals, this meant he was seen as one of the most gifted painters of his day, if not *the* most gifted.

Trained by his father, an engraver, to sketch fauna at an early age, the young Landseer showed considerable natural talent and was exhibiting works at the Royal Academy by the age of 13. Although a Londoner by birth, Landseer was a great enthusiast for the scenery of the Scottish Highlands, which forms the backdrop to many of his best-known works. He was a particularly keen painter of deer, and his masterpiece, *Monarch of the Glen* (1851) – a magnificent stag in noble pose – earned him enduring fame.

Landseer's admirers liked to say that he imbued his animals not only with character, but also with moral force. His abilities as an artist were so respected that vaguely supernatural stories began circulating regarding his works. Landseer was said, for instance, to be able to paint two separate subjects simultaneously, one with his left hand, the other with his right.

His considerable creative skills also extended to sculpture. During the construction of Trafalgar Square, Landseer modelled the four bronze lions that now sit at the foot of Nelson's Column. His painted works were highly popular and – distributed in the form of engravings made by his brother, Thomas – found their way into many Victorian homes.

Landseer's patrons included Queen Victoria and Prince Albert, who shared his enthusiasm for the Highlands; Victoria even knighted him. Sadly, in later life, Edwin Landseer succumbed to madness. The artist and sculptor was buried in St Paul's Cathedral.

LORD FREDERIC LEIGHTON
(1830–1896)
Painter, sculptor and pillar of the establishment

The first artist ever to be ennobled, albeit on the day before he died, Lord Frederic Leighton was one of the most prominent establishment figures of the Victorian age. His work, as one would expect from a man of such respectability and eminence, focused on historical and classical themes; many of his best-known paintings took their inspiration from stories in the Bible.

As a painter, Leighton worked in a highly finished style, favouring grand compositional schemes full of athletic bodies and strong colours. Many of his works were colossal in scale – *Cimabue's Celebrated Madonna is Carried in Procession through the Streets of Florence*, the piece that made his name, measured 17 feet across. As a painter, he could be seen as a considerable success, but as a sculptor he was less able.

A lifelong bachelor, Leighton is reputed to have been the model for his friend George Bernard Shaw's character of Professor Higgins in *Pygmalion*. When he died in 1896, Leighton was buried in St Paul's Cathedral.

CHARLES RENNIE MACKINTOSH
(1868–1928)
Architect and interior designer

Born in Glasgow, the city where he lived for most of his life, Charles Rennie Mackintosh became one of the principals of a particular branch of the Arts and Crafts movement – known in Europe as the Art Nouveau style – that flourished in Scotland towards the end of the Victorian age. Mackintosh suffered considerably in childhood from problems with his eyes that limited his ability to attend school so he spent his time learning how to draw.

Mackintosh became a draughtsman in an architectural practice, and earned his living from architecture throughout his life. He designed several buildings, including the Glasgow School of Art, but found it difficult to get many of his more ambitious projects off the ground. Painting in watercolours alongside two sisters, Margaret and Frances Macdonald, and a friend named Herbert MacNair, he formed a group known as the Glasgow Four to work in their new style. The quartet became romantically as well as artistically entangled; MacNair married Frances Macdonald and Mackintosh wed Margaret in 1900.

Mackintosh's interest in the exteriors of buildings extended to a fascination with their interiors and he designed furniture and fittings to the smallest of details – his outsize ladder-back chair is considered a design classic. Mackintosh's most lasting contribution to Scottish art was his interpretation of Art Nouveau, featuring heavy oriental influences and an eye for colour.

JOHN EVERETT MILLAIS
(1829–1896)
Pre-Raphaelite portrait painter

A child prodigy who became the youngest pupil ever to enrol at the Royal Academy of Art in London, John Everett Millais was one of the most significant figures in the Pre-Raphaelite Brotherhood. Later on he became not only the most commercially successful artist of the 19th century, but also the first to be created a baronet.

Born in Southampton, Millais exhibited such precocious ability as an artist that his family moved to London when he was nine in order to further his education. Admitted to the Royal Academy at just 11 years of age, the young Millais, known to fellow students as 'The Child', experienced considerable bullying, but he also made several lifelong friends. Among those he first met at the academy were Dante Gabriel Rossetti and William Holman Hunt, the men with whom he was to found the controversial Pre-Raphaelite Brotherhood.

Rejecting the wisdom of the day, which saw Raphael as supreme among artists, the new school was influenced by the art and architecture of the medieval period and, in particular, by religious iconography; at the same time, they sought to bring naturalism to historical subjects. Charles Dickens was horrified by Millais' painting *Christ in the House of His Parents*, which eschewed convention by portraying Mary and Joseph as ordinary human beings, calling Millais' Jesus 'a hideous wry-necked blubbering boy'.

It was the need to earn money, not the strictures of a critic, that forced Millais to change his style. Having grown accustomed to painting at a glacial pace in difficult media – typically preparing backgrounds during the summer and adding figures during the winter – the artist was forced to concede he was unable to earn a living painting an area 'no larger than a five-shilling piece' each day. His new style, considerably more dramatic, was in tune with the sentimental tastes of the mid-Victorian period, but has since been condemned as being somewhat 'chocolate-boxy'. However, at the time his change in style began to make him a lot of money – at the peak of his career he earned as much as £30,000 a year. He painted a number of 'imperial' works, including a study of a dying Disraeli, and was knighted in 1885.

In person, Millais was a quintessential Victorian, boyishly enthusiastic, bushy-bearded and devoted in equal measure to field sports and his family. His wife, Effie, was the former spouse of John Ruskin (it was

rumoured that Ruskin never consummated the marriage). Millais and
Effie had eight children. Always a heavy smoker, Millais died of throat
cancer shortly after succeeding Frederick Leighton as president of the
Royal Academy.

WILLIAM MORRIS
(1834–1896)
*Wallpaper designer, socialist and creator of the
British Arts and Crafts Movement*

Born in the London suburb of Walthamstow to a well-off family, William
Morris could easily have obeyed the father who wished him to become
a churchman. Instead, he decided to embark upon a career as an artist, a
career that led him to reject almost all of his earliest influences.

Having earned a precarious living as a painter for five years, Morris
turned to design in 1862, founding the firm that would become renowned
as Morris & Company, and making a name for himself as a designer of
wallpaper and domestic interiors.

His central belief – that mass production was destroying the traditional
craftsmanship that was an ennobling activity for the common man – drove
him to make a fetish of old-fashioned crafts and all that was handmade. His
hatred of the evils of large-scale manufacturing and the degraded lives it
forced on the workers maintaining the machines prompted him to become an
active socialist.

Morris knew and worked closely with many of the central figures in the
art world of the day, including Edward Burne-Jones and Dante Gabriel
Rossetti, and in the course of his long career displayed a startling array
of talents. He created furniture, wove tapestries, published fantasy and
socialist utopian novels, wrote medieval-style poetry, and even translated
an acclaimed Icelandic saga. His Kelmscott Press set new standards in
typography and book design. However, it is as a designer and printer

of intricate, hand-drawn wallpapers that William Morris is perhaps best remembered. A great many of his best-loved designs are still licensed and manufactured. As a confirmed socialist, Morris worked closely with Friedrich Engels and Karl Marx's daughter, Eleanor, to build a workers' movement in Britain, although he failed in his attempts to mediate between the Marxist and anarchist factions that soon developed in his socialist league.

JOSEPH PAXTON
(1801–1865)
Gardener, architect and creator of the Crystal Palace

Born into a life of considerable poverty in Woburn, Bedfordshire, Joseph Paxton received almost no schooling and seemed to have very few prospects. But all that would change. At the age of 15, he went to work on his brother's farm where, starved and badly beaten, he soon ran away and chose to make his way in the world as a practical gardener, joining the staff of the Duke of Devonshire.

A chance meeting in the gardens brought the young man to the attention of the duke and, impressed by his obvious intelligence, Devonshire impulsively offered Paxton the post of foreman of his arboretum in Chiswick. The two men swiftly became friends and Paxton was managing no fewer than six large estates by the 1840s. While still in the duke's employ, he branched out into architecture, designing a conservatory and lily house at Chatsworth in Derbyshire, and building the vast Emperor Fountain – the largest in Europe.

These experiences emboldened Paxton sufficiently for him to attempt work on an even more monumental scale, specifically the vast Crystal Palace erected in Hyde Park for the Great Exhibition of 1851. The design of this revolutionary structure is said to have been inspired by the gigantic South American water lilies grown at Chatsworth, which prompted Paxton

to experiment with rigid, radiating iron ribs until he was able to build large
structures that appeared to be almost entirely made of glass.

Paxton, who drew up the plans on blotting paper in a mere nine days,
personally oversaw construction. Built by 200 men in less than eight
months, Paxton took care to ensure that what was planned to be a temporary
structure would be as easy to disassemble as it had been to put up.

Nothing remotely like it had been seen before. The Crystal Palace was
1,850 feet long, 450 feet wide and more than 100 feet high, and used
nearly 300,000 panes of glass. The huge crowds attracted to the Great
Exhibition were overwhelmed by the lightness of the structure and, when
the Exhibition drew to a close, it was decided to reassemble the entire
structure south of the Thames, in Sydenham, where it gave its name to an
entire district.

For his achievement Joseph Paxton was knighted, and in time became
a Liberal MP. His fantastic Crystal Palace outlived him, standing until it
burned down in 1936.

AUGUSTUS PUGIN
(1812–1852)
*Architect and critic who designed the interiors
for the Houses of Parliament*

A London architect by trade, Augustus Pugin gained renown as one of the
principal designers of the present Houses of Parliament, built beside
the River Thames to replace an earlier structure that burnt down in 1833.
Pugin was born to a French Protestant draughtsman who trained his son to
illustrate Gothic buildings for his books. He grew up to be notably religious,
converting to Roman Catholicism while in his 20s and objecting to the
prevailing neo-classical style of the day on the grounds that it was pagan.
Pugin argued in *True Principles of Christian Architecture*, that the Gothic
style was the one best calculated to please God.

Pugin's early training was as a furniture maker and theatrical stage designer, and it was the latter that led him to train as an architect. His greatest coup was to be called in by Charles Barry, who had won a competition to design the new Houses of Parliament; Pugin asked to complete Barry's half-finished drawings for the project. This commission gave him considerable leeway to add ornamentation to the exterior of the building and florid detail to the barely sketched-out interiors. In the opinion of the critic AN Wilson, Pugin had a lasting effect on British national character thanks to his efforts with the Houses of Parliament. 'There is no doubt,' Wilson wrote, 'that the British would think differently if their parliamentary buildings resembled the Assembleé Nationale in Paris or the Senate in Washington.'

Throughout his life, Pugin had a great love of the sea, and generally dressed in sailors' jackets and loose trousers. He had a considerable work ethic, often working from dawn until midnight with little rest, to the despair of the trio of wives (married in succession) who bore him a total of eight children. He died at 40 of a stroke, brought on, it has been argued, by mercury poisoning.

JOSEPH MALLORD TURNER
(1775–1851)
Sea and landscape painter

A Londoner – he was born in Covent Garden – and the son of a wigmaker-turned-barber-surgeon, Joseph Mallord Turner was largely self-taught as an artist. He exhibited an equal mastery of watercolours and oils, revolutionised painting with his extraordinary use of light, and prefigured the style that would become known, almost half a century after his death, as Impressionism.

Turner received little formal schooling, but exhibited early signs of promise as an artist. First expressing an interest in painting during a stay in Brentford, he began to create canvases that his father displayed in the windows of his shop. He applied to the Royal Academy of Art at the age of 14 and was accepted after an interview conducted by Sir Joshua Reynolds. Turner also showed an early interest in architectural drawing, but began to exhibit in oils after 1796. The painter travelled widely in Europe after 1802, and showed little fear of incorporating new discoveries and new styles into his work.

His greatest successes included *The Fighting Temeraire* (1839), depicting an old-fashioned battleship, the 98-gun *Temeraire*, being towed to the breaker's yard by a new steam-powered tugboat. Another work – *Rain, Steam and Speed* (1844) – is a dramatically impressionistic vision of the motion of a railway engine tearing across a stormy landscape. In planning this picture, Turner famously had himself strapped to the front of a locomotive as it steamed out of London, displaying, at the age of 69, a commitment to observational veracity few of his successors have found it necessary to emulate.

Despite his renowned body of work, the painter's private life is a mystery. He never married, preferring to keep a mistress, and eschewed close company. He lived and worked with his father who became his assistant for almost 30 years. He died, aged 76, in temporary lodgings under the name of Booth.

FRANZ WINTERHALTER
(1806–1873)
Queen Victoria's favourite artist

A German-born portrait artist who earned acclaim in Paris, Franz Winterhalter came to Britain on numerous occasions in order to paint members of the royal family. He was also reputed to be Queen Victoria's favourite painter. Well-bred and well-educated, he was sufficiently ingratiating to make a success of painting subjects of the nobility, including the queen herself.

Winterhalter was renowned for his ability to capture likenesses that, while flattering, were nearly exact, so that his oeuvre, while poorly regarded for a long time from a purely artistic perspective, has always been considered a valuable historical resource.

In keeping with his elevated social position, Winterhalter led a personal life of considerable probity. One curiosity that was often commented upon was the injury that he suffered to his right hand quite early on in his career. With effort, the resourceful artist was able to learn to paint equally well with his left, and was commonly said, in time, to have come to prefer it to his right.

JOHN WOLFE-BARRY
(1836–1919)
Civil engineer who designed and constructed Tower Bridge

John Wolfe-Barry's father, Sir Charles Barry, was a noted architect whose triumphs included the Reform Club in London and the new Palace of Westminster. So perhaps it was inevitable that his son, John, would follow in his footsteps.

Wolfe-Barry built a career that was solid but hardly distinguished until, in his late 40s, a census conducted in the summer of 1882 showed that the average traffic passing over London Bridge, which was 54 feet wide, each day amounted to more than 22,000 vehicles and nearly 111,000 pedestrians. A decision was taken to construct a new bridge further downstream in order to relieve the traffic. Wolfe-Barry and his associates were determined to enter the competition to design this new structure.

The problem confronting any would-be designers was that the site chosen bisected the Pool of London, the highest navigable portion of the River Thames for seagoing ships. Therefore, the new bridge would have to be designed in order to permit access for shipping bound for their time-honoured moorings. A large number of potential designs were considered and the winning entry, which became Tower Bridge, was submitted by Horace Jones, the City architect, and Wolfe-Barry. It called for the incorporation of bascules (spans capable of being raised and lowered) to admit tall ships to the Pool.

An Act of Parliament approving construction of the new bridge was passed in 1885 and the work was eventually completed (well behind schedule) in 1894, at a cost of £1 million. Wolfe-Barry's assistant on the project was Isambard Brunel, son of the celebrated engineer Isambard Kingdom Brunel, and their completed structure almost immediately became an icon of London.

The most telling indication that Wolfe-Barry's design was a success is the fact that the large passenger lifts built into the structure to take pedestrians to walkways on the upper levels, are practically never used; the bridge's users prefer to wait the few minutes it takes to raise and lower the bascules instead.

CHAPTER XII

GOOD SPORTS

CHARLES ALCOCK
(1842–1907)
Footballer and administrator known as 'The father of modern sport'

Born in Sunderland and educated at Harrow, an amateur footballer who did more than any other man to create the all-professional Football League, Charles Alcock was a study in contradictions successfully resolved.

Although perhaps best known today as the long-serving secretary of the Football Association (FA) during its critical early years from 1870 to 1895, Alcock was also a prolific journalist, a noted publisher and a keen cricketer who, in 1880, arranged the first-ever Test match between England and Australia. As a footballer, Alcock captained Wanderers FC – the Chelsea of the early 1870s – to victory in the first-ever FA Cup final. As an administrator, his innovations included international football; he was the mastermind behind the first official England versus Scotland fixture in 1872.

Astonishingly productive even by Victorian standards, Alcock combined his writing career and administrative role at the FA with the secretaryship of Surrey County Cricket Club, where he was responsible for the building of the Kennington Oval. At the time of its completion, the Oval was – thanks to Alcock's love of virtually every sport – not only a major cricketing ground, but also the UK national centre for lacrosse, baseball, cycling, athletics and even roller-skating.

JAMES CARR-BOYLE, 5TH EARL OF GLASGOW
(1792–1869)
Magnificent, if dangerously eccentric, racehorse owner

Many wealthy aristocrats have been devoted to racing, but few have had as little success as the 5th Earl of Glasgow, whose lifelong love of the turf left him with little to show by way of either prize money or prized studs. Part of the problem was Carr-Boyle's reluctance to give any of his horses names, a habit that naturally caused great confusion in the stables. The earl also proved obstinately devoted to several bloodlines 'of proved uselessness', and his notoriously vile temper hindered plans for the long-term development of the few promising animals that he did possess. It was common for Carr-Boyle to order that horses which had failed to live up to expectations on the daily gallops be shot on the spot. His record, one despairing trainer noted, was six summary executions in a single morning.

The eccentric earl proved equally dangerous when hunting. When unable to flush out any foxes, he was quite likely to arbitrarily designate one of his own huntsmen as the quarry and relentlessly pursue the unfortunate individual across the countryside for miles.

LOTTIE DOD
(1871–1960)
Youngest-ever winner of a Wimbledon singles title

Born into one of the most talented sporting families in England, Charlotte 'Lottie' Dod decided to take up tennis at the age of nine and won the women's singles championship at Wimbledon only six years later at the tender age of 15. Dod remains the youngest woman ever to secure this particular accolade.

Playing, as was the custom of the time, in long sleeves, full-length skirts and heavy boots, Dod was one of only six women to enter the Wimbledon tournament of 1887. She defeated the reigning champion, Blanche Bingley, 6-2, 6-0 in the final. She maintained an active social life that prevented her from entering the tournament in 1889 and caused her to take an entire year off from tennis a year later, yet she won at Wimbledon five times and lost only five matches in her entire career.

During this time Dod caused a minor sensation by becoming the first woman to play a major tournament wearing a calf-length skirt, which she adapted from her school uniform.

A keen and phenomenally talented sportswoman, Dod also played hockey for Britain, won the women's national golf championship, and represented her country at archery in the 1908 Olympic Games. During the winter months she tobogganed down the famous Cresta Run and took up mountaineering. Today, Dod is widely regarded as one of the two or three most versatile sportswomen of all time. She died, aged 88, listening to a radio commentary from Wimbledon.

JOHN SHOLTO DOUGLAS, 9TH MARQUESS OF QUEENSBURY (1844–1900)
Creator of the Queensbury Rules and father of Oscar Wilde's boyfriend

Few members of the British aristocracy have been quite so unpopular as the 9th Marquess of Queensbury, an avid sportsman whose boorishness alienated the majority of his peers. Queensbury is best remembered for sponsoring a new code of rules for boxing, which provided for the use of gloves, three-minute rounds and defined what should be considered a fair fight. As the new rules gained in popularity, the far more brutal sport of bare-knuckle boxing declined.

Boxing was, however, only one of Douglas's keen interests. Unusually for the time, the marquess was a determined atheist who refused to participate in the 'Christian tomfoolery' of taking the traditional oath of allegiance to his sovereign and was consequently barred from taking a seat in the House of Lords. In 1882, he was ejected from a performance of Alfred, Lord Tennyson's play *The Promise of May* after loudly objecting to the chief villain of the piece being portrayed as an especially unpleasant atheist.

Douglas's final brush with fame came in 1895, when he discovered that his son, Lord Alfred Douglas, was being pursued by Oscar Wilde.

The marquess left a card, addressed to: 'Oscar Wilde, posing as a somdomite' [sic] at the writer's club. Wilde sued for libel, lost, and was later convicted of gross indecency and imprisoned for a year in Reading Gaol (see chapter VII).

WG GRACE
(1848–1915)
Legendary batsman and 'kidnapper'

No man has ever cast so long a shadow over the game of cricket as the portly, but undoubtedly brilliant, Dr William Gilbert Grace. Supreme skill as a batsman secured Grace all manner of records. At his peak, in the 1870s, he regularly averaged scores of between 60 and 70 runs, this at a time when rough and uncovered pitches made high scoring a much trickier proposition than it is today.

Some of his cricketing accolades include making 344 for Marylebone Cricket Club (MCC) against Kent in 1876, scoring 10 double centuries, and in 1895, at the age of 46, hitting 1,000 runs in May. But perhaps the good doctor's most extraordinary and unusual record was the one he claimed for the longest shot – 36 miles – after striking a ball onto a passing steam train.

WG, as he was universally known, was also one of cricket's greatest showmen. Playing on one occasion against a Cheltenham XI the doctor agreed to bat with a broomstick and still made 35 runs; on another occasion, he supposedly declined to 'walk' after being bowled with the first ball, arguing that the crowd had come to watch him bat.

The modern image of Grace as a rather plump bearded figure – he played well into his 50s – belies the considerable athleticism he displayed while in his prime. However, he was also a renowned gamesman, a quality he notoriously displayed in 'kidnapping' the great batsman Billy Midwinter when the latter was due to turn out for the Australians in 1878. Grace insisted that Midwinter play a fixture for his county, Gloucestershire, instead, and forcibly removed the player from Lords to the Oval to do so. Midwinter reluctantly complied with the wishes of his county skipper, but got his revenge, scoring 4 and 0 in his two innings.

JOHN JAQUES II
(1795–1867)
Genius who popularised croquet and invented Snakes & Ladders

Most men would be extremely content with the fame attached to introducing one great game to the world, but not John Jaques II, the London-based grandson of a French Huguenot ivory turner. Aside from introducing and popularising the ancient sport of croquet – a game for which he quite literally wrote the rules – Jaques was also a prolific inventor of card and board games, which he marketed via his family firm. Among his creations are the perennially popular Happy Families, Tiddlywinks, Ludo and Snakes & Ladders. He also pioneered a now-forgotten variant of table bowls called Squails, where players had to hit discs with the heel of their hand from the edge of the table towards a jack in the middle.

Jaques, who was heavily involved in the promotion of dominos and draughts, found time to display his various creations at the Great Exhibition of 1851 and the popularity of croquet as an English garden party pastime is generally dated to around this time. In 1869, the great man was rewarded with the title of Freeman of the City of London.

Innovation evidently ran in the family. Jaques' son, John III, is generally credited with the invention of Gossima, the forerunner of table tennis. John IV, meanwhile, was employed during World War II in making 'escape kits' to be smuggled into prisoner-of-war camps. Aptly, his creations included cribbage boards and other games paraphernalia with secret map compartments.

THE RIGHT HONOURABLE ARTHUR KINNAIRD, 11TH LORD KINNAIRD
(1847–1923)

*Aristocratic footballer, five-time FA Cup winner
and long-serving president of the Football Association*

E ven today, nearly 130 years after his retirement, no man has ever played
on the winning side in more FA Cup finals than Lord Kinnaird, one
of the founding fathers of the Association game and arguably the leading
player in the world during the 1870s.

The lavishly red-bearded aristocrat represented Wanderers FC in the
second-ever FA Cup final in 1873, and won three titles with the club before
switching his allegiance to Old Etonians. He won the Cup with them on two
further occasions, standing on his head in front of the pavilion to celebrate his
fifth and last winners' medal in 1882. In the course of his nine FA Cup finals
he played in every position, from forward to goalkeeper, while simultaneously
serving as treasurer and later president of the Football Association.

Showered with honours though he was, this superb sportsman also picked
up at least one unwanted distinction. He scored the first significant own
goal in football history while keeping goal for Wanderers FC against Oxford
University in the Cup final of 1877. He had accidentally stepped back between
his own posts and over the goal line while preparing to punt the ball clear.

In later years it would often – rather unfairly, some might say – be alleged
that, as a particularly influential figure on the FA council, Kinnaird attempted
to suppress this rather embarrassing incident by having the official record
expunged and the score changed from 2-1 to Wanderers to 2-0.

Kinnaird continued to play football into his mid-40s and was always
respected as a tough opponent. When his anxious wife once confided to a
friend that she feared her husband would come home one day with a broken
leg, the friend, who knew Kinnaird well, responded: 'You must not worry,
madam. If he does, it will not be his own.'

OLD TOM MORRIS
(1821–1908)
Pioneering golfer who helped to create the 18-hole game

Perhaps being born in St Andrews, the spiritual home of golf, had something to do with it, but Tom Morris always seemed destined to become one of the great figures in the history of the game.

He started young, working as an apprentice for Allan Robertson, the man generally regarded as the first golf professional; he soon began making a living playing for bets and manufacturing and selling clubs and balls.

In later life, Morris became perhaps the first professional course designer in the world, charging customers such as the Muirfield and Carnoustie clubs £1 a day for his services. Among Morris's more decisive interventions was the part he played in reducing the famed St Andrews course from 23 holes to 18, creating a model that has been followed ever since.

Morris was a four-time Open champion, and still holds records as the oldest player to win the Open (he was 46 when he took glory in 1867) and as winner by the largest margin in the history of the tournament – 13 strokes in 1862. Morris's son, known as 'Young' Tom Morris, also became a champion golfer and the two are said never to have been beaten while playing as a pair. Morris remained an active golfer well into his 80s. He died of a fractured skull sustained falling down some stairs at the St Andrews clubhouse.

ALFRED MYNN
(1807–1861)
Noted cricketer and serial bankrupt, first of the great fast bowlers

Alfred Mynn was, without doubt, the greatest cricketer of the first half of the 19th century. Weighing in during his prime at around 20 stone and standing over six feet tall, he towered over most of his contemporaries and was widely known as 'The Lion of Kent'.

Mynn came to maturity just as the cricketing authorities legalised overarm bowling, and used his size to great advantage, becoming probably the fastest and most accurate bowler of the 1830s. His prowess made him a target for other players, a dangerous proposition in the days when many players spurned pads. In the North versus South match of 1836, Mynn was struck repeatedly on the shin by the almost equally fast Samuel Redgate, sustaining such serious injuries that for a while it was feared his leg would have to be amputated. Thankfully, he recovered, his restorative powers being attributed by contemporaries to his healthy appetite.

The son of a hop farmer, Mynn was renowned as a hearty eater and heavy drinker. He would habitually consume a huge roast and take a full tankard of ale to bed with him on the night before a key match on the grounds that: 'Beef and beer are the things to play cricket on.' However, the fabulous bowler was less successful in his private life, being bankrupted several times and even having to serve a short term in a debtors' prison. Mynn was memorably eulogised after his death in an epitaph by WJ Prowse that still graces his gravestone in the little village of Thurnham. It reads:

All were proud of him, all loved him… As the changing seasons pass,
As our champion lies a-sleeping underneath the Kentish grass,
Proudly, sadly we will name him – to forget him were a sin –
Lightly lie the turf upon thee, kind and manly Alfred Mynn.

TOM SAYERS
(1826–1865)
Bare-knuckle prizefighter

They called him 'The Little Wonder', and it was a title that he certainly earned. Tom Sayers, who stood only five feet eight inches tall and weighed under 11 stone, was perhaps the last great bare-knuckle boxing champion of England. He held the title from 1858 to 1860, battling the

American champion, John C Heenan, for the championship of the world, the first time such an honour had been formally contested.

Born in Brighton, Sayers left school at 13, still illiterate, and became an apprentice bricklayer. He spent most of his 11-year career fighting men considerably bigger than himself, yet lost only one bout. Bricklaying built up his fists and The Little Wonder was particularly renowned for his exceptionally sharp knuckles, a significant advantage in the days before gloves became compulsory.

Sayers' first win, on a muddy Wandsworth Common, was over an Irish navvy who stood six feet three inches tall. The Little Wonder, fighting in bare feet, stayed with his opponent for two hours and 20 minutes until the mud clinging to the latter's boots began to slow him down. Sayer later defeated William Perry, 'The Tipton Slasher', to win the English heavyweight title. Sayers' match with Heenan, lasting well over two hours, was ruled a draw, although the American was left in a critical condition and spent two days recovering in a darkened room. Sayers' backers then persuaded him to retire.

But the champion's private life was unhappy; his wife was unfaithful to him, bearing at least four children by a lover, and Sayers drank heavily to drown his sorrows after his retirement, ending his life as a virtual alcoholic. Aristocratic patrons raised £3,000 for the champion and he lived on that small fortune until his death, from tuberculosis, at the age of only 39.

GILBERT OSWALD SMITH
(1872–1943)
Gentleman centre-forward who refused, as a matter of principle,
ever to head the ball

Weedy and asthmatic he may have been, but Gilbert Oswald Smith was also the first great English centre-forward. Known to everyone as 'GO' – the footballing equivalent of cricket's 'WG' (Grace) – he worked on his game until he was perhaps the finest passer of the ball in the country and was deadly in front of goal. Smith scored a goal every other game for England, a remarkable total for someone who could scarcely be described as a complete centre-forward since it was widely rumoured that he refused ever to muddy his forehead by actually heading the ball. At a time when each team played only three internationals a year, Smith, a Charterhouse and Oxford man, accumulated a total of 21 England caps in a career that spanned well over a decade, the record total at the time. He was also a stalwart of the famous Corinthians team, an amateur ensemble formed to represent all that was best about the game.

Smith played his whole career as an amateur, which at that time meant keeping a polite distance from the professionals, or 'players'. Some of the 'gentlemen' on the England team proved more patrician than other individuals – Charles Wreford Brown, for example, who captained the side in Smith's day, used to carry a supply of gold sovereigns onto the field in a deep pocket and press one into the hand of each proletarian goal scorer when the ball went in – but Smith was always respected by his working-class colleagues. 'He was the finest type of amateur,' his striking partner, Steve Bloomer, observed, 'one who would always shake hands with us professionals in a manner which said plainly he was pleased to meet them.'

After retiring from the game, Smith became headmaster of Ludgrove School in Barnet, where he tutored new generations of players.

ARTHUR WHARTON
(1865–1930)
World record-setting sprinter and first black professional footballer

Born on the Gold Coast (now Ghana) to a Scottish father and a mother who was a member of the local royal family, Arthur Wharton came to Britain in the early 1880s to train as a missionary, a vocation he soon abandoned for that of professional sportsman.

Always lightning-quick on his feet, Wharton managed to set a new world record – 10 seconds – for the 100-yard dash in July 1886, shone as a cyclist and even played professional cricket. He was most renown, however, as a footballer, appearing in goal for a succession of semi-professional and professional clubs between 1884 and 1902.

Wharton was not the first black man to play football in Britain – that distinction belongs to the Queens Park amateur Andrew Watson – but he was the first to do so professionally, overcoming considerable institutional racism to claim a place in the starting line-ups of some of the best North of England sides of the day. Wharton proved himself an athletic and showy goalkeeper, capable of some of the most astonishing saves. One spectator who saw him play for Rotherham in the late 1880s recalled an incident in which Wharton leapt up, grabbed the crossbar with both hands, and saved a shot by clamping the ball between his knees, hauling himself out of the way just in time to avoid three onrushing forwards who ended up in an ignominious heap inside the goal.

For all his athleticism, though, Wharton was unlucky in his moves from club to club, leaving Preston North End just as the team embarked on what would become the first-ever league and cup double. He later transferred to Sheffield United just as the even more celebrated keeper William 'Fatty' Foulke was coming into his prime. Foulke's larger-than-life physique kept Wharton from seeing first-team action during his time there. Later on, Wharton worked, almost forgotten, as a coal miner in Rotherham. He died penniless, apparently of syphilis, and was buried in an unmarked grave. It was not until 1997 that his grave was rediscovered and a more fitting headstone and tribute was erected.